A Playbook for Habitual Excellence:
A Leader's Roadmap From the
Life and Work of Paul H. O'Neill, Sr.

Published by Value Capture, LLC.

Edited by Mark Graban and Melissa Moore

Edition September 23, 2020

Profound change. Sustainable results.

First edition

ISBN 9798674997849

Published by Value Capture, LLC

www.ValueCaptureLLC.com

12 Federal St #100
One North Shore Center
Pittsburgh, PA 15212

Also available in Kindle format and as a free PDF
eBook: www.ValueCaptureLLC.com/playbook

Table of Contents

About Paul H. O'Neill, Sr.

Adapted from www.pauloneilllegacy.com.

Paul O'Neill (1935–2020) would often say that, in any human organization:

> **"With leadership, anything is possible, and without it, nothing is possible."**

Paul O'Neill, a true leader, personified this observation.

He inspired and guided others to achieve some of the most important accomplishments of the last 50 years in business, healthcare, education, and government. To Paul, however, the remarkable feats he led or impacted were demonstrations meant to show every person involved, and each of us, that we could do it too, in everything that mattered. He challenged us all to be unafraid to tap into our natural aspiration to be great and to accomplish things together that our country and communities so desperately need.

To name just a few examples of Paul's leadership legacy and influence:

- From 1987 to 2000, as CEO of Alcoa, he led the once-troubled aluminum giant to become the world's safest organization, while increasing its market size by 800%. He showed that a strategy anchored in values and something that mattered more than making aluminum — safety —

could unleash remarkable performance across more than 140,000 people around the globe.

- As the head of the domestic section of (what is now) the Office of Management and Budget under President Gerald Ford, he had a leading hand in many of the most important domestic policy advances for decades. These include not only pivotal programs such as Medicare and the Veterans Administration health system, but the creation of the nation's first budgeting system that linked federal investments to the actual value they produced for citizens, called outcomes-based budgeting. Later, as Treasury Secretary of the United States, he shepherded the U.S. financial system through the shock of the 9/11 attacks and their aftermath, and stood on principles, as always, even though it ultimately cost him his position.

- Paul, as a volunteer, taught and energized the spread of the safety and operational excellence movements to healthcare, personally inspiring some of the earliest proof that long-accepted injuries and rates of medical error could be eliminated, the quality of medical outcomes could be dramatically increased, and the wastefulness that drives up the costs of care eliminated.

As proof after proof emerged, Paul espoused his foundational *sine qua non* of excellence and urged us to use it. It started with a simple trilogy of questions that every person in an organization should be able to answer affirmatively every day, without reservation:

- Am I treated with dignity and respect by everyone I encounter without regard to race, gender, rank, educational attainment, or any other distinguishing feature?

- Am I given the tools, training, resources, encouragement, etc., to make a contribution to the organization that adds meaning to my life?

- Am I recognized for that contribution by someone whose opinion matters to me?

Throughout his career and personal life, Paul lived according to his principles. Some examples include:

- Unshakable integrity. A clear sense of right and wrong, and acting on it.

- Relentlessly driving out any force that would demean or divide people based on any difference such as race, sexual preference, level of education, or any other differentiator.

- Tapping into the human aspiration to excel, challenging ourselves to be the best in the world at everything we do. To aspire to achieve "the theoretical limit." As he said, "If God didn't decree we can't do it via the laws of physics, anything is possible."

- Transparency and taking direct ownership as the leader for things gone wrong.

- Passionately promoting practical, scientifically-based, data-indicated approaches to getting better every day, focusing where people are doing the real work that helps other people, not sitting around in fancy offices.

Paul saw it as a sacred leadership responsibility to aspire to perfection and create the conditions where people could collectively come amazingly close to achieving perfection by solving practical problems every day. He saw people as unworthy of leadership roles if they were unwilling to transparently hold themselves accountable to this standard.

Accomplishments like those achieved by people who were inspired and guided by Paul O'Neill are within each of us, and all of us together. Paul O'Neill taught us the way.

Paul O'Neill touched and inspired people from all walks of life, in many sectors, all over the world.

Foreword

By John S. Toussaint M.D., founder and chairman of Catalysis

Great leaders lead from a bedrock of core values and principles. They are easy to spot. They set a clear and attainable vision. They don't blame — instead, they take responsibility for problems. They are positive. They are relentless in the pursuit of excellence. They value their staff over everything else, including finances. Sound familiar? There is no better example of such a leader than Paul O'Neill. His bedrock was his family, his faith, and a set of well-articulated principles.

I first met Paul at an Institute for Healthcare Improvement (IHI) meeting in the early 2000s. It was a meeting on patient safety. All he could talk about was employee safety. I didn't understand why he was talking about that at a patient safety meeting. It would take me ten years to finally understand that patient safety starts with employee safety. Without employee safety, there can be no commitment to safety at all.

At the core, Paul believed in the principle of respect for people. He started many conversations with questions like these:

- Can every one of your staff say yes to the statement of "I am respected by everyone every day at work"?
- Have you as a leader created an environment that allows people to do work that gives their life meaning?
- Have you thanked people for the good work they have done?

The best test of respect is if it's safe for me to go to work every day. When Paul took over at Alcoa, it was far from a safe place to work. In fact, young men were dying in the plants as he eloquently recalled with riveting detail. Paul was disgusted by this and it caused him to relentlessly pursue a safe work environment for everyone. Work injuries and deaths were not compatible with the fundamental principles that guided him.

One of the truly great stories that has stuck with me is that of the phone number, as you will hear him talk about in this book. Paul went to the plant in Alcoa, Tennessee, and told the employees to call him at home if there was ever a safety problem that wasn't being addressed. He gave them his home phone number.

A few weeks later, he received a call from a worker late one evening. The worker said there were large ingots that they had to move by hand because a section of roller conveyor had been broken for days. It took many men to move an ingot and the worker was pretty sure someone would be injured.

Paul thanked the worker and immediately called the plant manager and woke him up. He instructed him to get down to the plant that night and fix the equipment. Paul said, "Call me when it's fixed." By morning, the equipment was working normally.

As Paul told the story, he described the "tom-tom" system of communication that echoed throughout the company. Every worker in every plant around the country quickly knew what had happened. This was the beginning of a remarkable story that shifted a company in a notoriously unsafe industry to the safest of all.

In this time of the Covid-19 pandemic, Paul's legacy has become even more real and important. Tens of thousands of healthcare workers have become infected — hundreds have died — mostly due to healthcare leadership shirking the responsibility of keeping staff safe.

On the other hand, a few organizations have had no one become infected, as Ken Segel (of Value Capture) and I recently wrote about for HBR.[1] If Paul were here, he would be proud of these organizations. He would want to go visit and see and bump elbows with this group of great leaders that all took his three questions to heart.

Let's consider what healthcare leaders and all leaders must do today to truly be living the legacy of Paul O'Neill.

First, set a goal of zero workplace injuries. That is what Paul did at Alcoa and he made that company the safest in the world for workers. Duke Health has done it during Covid-19 and has achieved zero staff infections as of June 15, 2020. Leaders delivered all the personal protective equipment where and when it was needed. Leaders had a relentless focus on keeping staff (and patients) safe. In fact, leaders and staff started safety huddles each morning by reciting a pledge to "commit to zero harm for our patients, their loved ones, and ourselves."

Second, staff safety must become the most important value in the organization. No other priority can take precedent. Torrance Memorial hospital in Los Angeles is a wonderful example. During Covid-19, instead of furloughing

[1] https://hbr.org/2020/06/health-care-workers-protect-us-its-time-to-protect-them

staff, leaders redeployed them to make face shields and disinfectant wipes and to check temperatures of staff and patients at the door. The mostly outpatient staff were thrilled — not only to have a job — but to be doing meaningful work that supported their colleagues in the ICU.

Third, make staff safety transparent. At Alcoa, everyone in the company knew when an injury occurred and what was done to make sure it never happened again. The same is true at International Hospital Corporation in Costa Rica. All injuries are reported in a daily report. Root cause analysis must be completed on injuries within 48 hours. New processes that assure the injury can't happen again are rapidly shared with everyone in the organization.

Fourth, create a daily management system that focuses on safety. This system should bubble up many problems. Safety problems should be the top priority. At Morningside Hospital, part of the Mt. Sinai health system in Manhattan, multiple daily huddles were occurring during Covid-19. Problems were quickly identified and addressed. After a patient was intubated, the respiratory arrest team reported back that the necessary PPE to protect the multiple members of the resuscitation team were not available. The huddle system led to the creation of PPE "bags-to-go." The bags contain enough full sets of PPE for nine people and are placed on the resuscitation carts.

Finally, don't use frontline caregiver heroism as an excuse not to act. Caregivers act heroically only when there are insufficient systems in place to support getting the work done. They must develop more and more workarounds like moving the ingot by hand because the conveyor was broken. Every workaround leads potentially to a safety problem. Leaders and managers must create a management system that immediately addresses worker problems and trains the front line to solve the problems themselves.

Paul Sr. gave many his unconditional love. As his son, Paul Jr., said at his memorial service, "He was my best friend." Paul was my friend, my mentor, and my inspiration. His faith and core principles guided him and helped him endure many obstacles along the way. He emerged stronger each time, never compromising on what he knew was right. What he gave the rest of us was hope that a life lived on the principle of respect can lead to unimaginable results in the lives of everyday working people.

John S. Toussaint, M
Appleton, Wisconsin
June 25, 2020

Preface and Acknowledgments

By Mark Graban, senior advisor for Value Capture and editor of this book

This book collects and shares transcripts of three speeches given by Paul H. O'Neill, Sr. between 2003 and 2014. Although the audiences were healthcare organizations, I believe that the approach that's laid out in these speeches is widely applicable to any type of organization or human endeavor.

Thanks are due to many, as, without their support and encouragement, this book would not exist.

We'd like to thank the organizations that gave the invitations and hosted the speeches that are captured here:

- UVA Health (at the invitation of Dr. Richard Shannon)
- Catalysis and the Lean Enterprise Institute
- The Institute for Healthcare Improvement
- Invited Testimony to the U.S. Senate Finance Committee

Thanks to UVA Health for sharing the video of the speech online,[2] and thanks to Catalysis and LEI for capturing and sharing audio[3] of the second speech that you'll read here. Additionally, many thanks to Vickie Pisowicz, a senior advisor with Value Capture, for transcribing the recorded IHI talk. Transcripts have been only

---

[2] https://vimeo.com/94451465
[3] https://bit.ly/3jwnt9k

very lightly edited in some instances. The transcripts are full and unabridged versions of the speeches.

Thanks also go to Value Capture's Helen Zak and Melissa Moore, for their support of this project and for their assistance along the way. I suggested creating this book because I hope the words and ideas captured here inspire you as much as they inspire me.

Thanks to you, the reader, for your time and attention.

Introduction

By Paul H. O'Neill, Jr.

I am pleased to be offering some thoughts as an introduction to this book, a collection of speeches by my father, Paul H. O'Neill, Sr.

This book exemplifies what Dad believed, that if you were willing to lead with a principled framework rooted in human aspiration to do important things, you could make a profound and measurable difference in people's lives. In these speeches, he is applying what he believed in healthcare settings. The core of his message is around safety not only for patients but for staff members as well. He gave speeches like this in many settings over the years, to the point where he delivered this message without notes at the University of Virginia (the first speech you'll read here).

I believe that, early on in his career at International Paper, he realized that worker safety could be a key driver for performance improvement. In his mind, if you said your employees were your most important asset, what better way to prove it than by building a leadership framework and system for every employee that made it possible to eliminate worker injuries in your workforce. This methodology could then be applied to all things that an organization tried to achieve in the pursuit of excellence. By the time he got to Alcoa, he knew what was possible and he proved it.

After his professional career ended, he proved the same thing as a volunteer, extending his influence to the largest sectors of our economy that have not been touched deeply enough by the pursuit of habitual excellence — education, and especially health care — at a great human cost.

Dad passed at a time when we were just learning that at least one of the healthcare leaders he counseled had produced a staff safety record that had finally passed Alcoa's on the way to zero, just as Alcoa had passed DuPont long ago. That is just as he would have wanted it. And he would be the first to remind us that should be the standard for every healthcare leader.

I would like to thank all of the people that worked on this project, including Value Capture team members Mark Graban, Melissa Moore, and Helen Zak, along with the executive chairman of Catalysis, John Toussaint, MD.

I know, in talking with Dad toward the end of his life, that he wanted all of us who know his story to continue the effort to expose as many people as possible to these leadership ideas and to assist those on a leadership journey to reach their fullest potential. This book is a part of that effort.

UVA Health (2014)

Introduction by Geoff Webster, co-founding principal of Value Capture

This speech was given a few months into the journey at UVA Health (part of the University of Virginia). Dr. Richard Shannon and Value Capture coordinated to schedule it at a moment when inspiration was needed and as a way to reinforce Dr. Shannon's vision to a much larger audience. This audience consisted of almost 600 people, constituting all levels of leadership of the medical center, medical school, nursing school, research apparatus, and health libraries. Before the speech, Paul visited a few nascent "model cells" and met many of the people who were leading UVA Health's continuous improvement efforts. Paul never wanted to give a speech without first making that connection and seeing what was really happening.

My hope today is that I can share with you some ideas that will be useful to you. One thing I've discovered in the things I've been privileged to do is how powerful it is to ask the questions that a third grader would ask.

When I go and speak, if I'm invited to go speak, to a third-grade class, it's the most daunting thing…

[laughter]

... because they ask questions that are so much harder than adults will ever ask you, in innocence. The questions I asked about the experts in heart surgery were childlike questions. They were offered in every good faith. I really wanted to know.

It's amazing to me what you can discover if you can put yourself back in that position where you're really seeking knowledge and you keep asking *why* until you're satisfied that you really have a grasp and an understanding.

Reducing Infections to Near Zero

I'm going to also say something as a little follow-up to what Rick said about the Pittsburgh Regional Healthcare Initiative. One of the things that we set out to do was to tackle the issue of central-line-associated bloodstream infections (CLABSIs).

After we dedicated ourselves to a proposition we should eliminate such infections, in 18 months in 44 hospitals in southwestern Pennsylvania the rate was reduced 67 percent. More directly to Rick's credit, he took these ideas at Allegheny and started expressing it simply as "the number of people with infections," so I'll tell you some numbers to illustrate this.

Rick was responsible for three units at Allegheny General Hospital if my memory serves me right. There were 1,753 patients in a year's time who went through these units.

Before the application of these ideas, like most places, they kept their facts in terms of infections per 1,000 line-days, which for the uneducated, it was a mystery to me. Why the hell would you express anything in terms of 1,000 line-days? Rick was into that, and so we converted the data from infections per 1,000 line-days to the simple question of:

"How many people got an infection?"

That was like a breakthrough.

The answer was, of 1,753 patients, 37 people got an infection, and 19 people died. It was better than the national average.

Somebody said, "Ooh, it was better than the national average." People took great comfort in that, "Well, we're as good as it's possible to be. Look at that. We're less than two percent. That's better than the national average."

Rick [Shannon] with these ideas, he didn't direct this. He enabled his people to become learners from data and from collaboration. They discovered some really interesting things. For one, all of the nurses had been trained in different places, and they were all sure that their way of doing things was the right way because that's how they learned it.

There were 37 different ways.

There was so much variability in the system it was damn near impossible to actually figure out how to have continuous improvement and learn from everything gone wrong.

Things that you all know here now were not so obvious to people 15 or 20 years ago. If you're going to do a central line, you need a prepackaged kit that's sterile. The gloves are on top so that you don't contaminate the stuff underneath on your way to the stuff underneath and you don't have to go search for a gown, or a glove, or a mask, or for the lines, all that stuff.

There's a way to prepare the [central line] site. Some people thought it was OK to use a certain kind of disinfectant. Other people thought something else. Some people thought you swabbed. Some people thought you swiped as you were preparing a site. There was so much variability. It seemed innocent but it wasn't really innocent.

Rick didn't tell them the answer. But together from their own observation and analysis, they figured it out. "This is the way we're going to do it. We're going to take the variability of this stuff out so that if there is an infection, we won't have all that underbrush to crawl through to try to figure out what break in protocol caused us to have an infection."

So 18 months later, they did a year's retrospective. They had 1,840 patients through those same three units. There was one infection and nobody died. Rick did that. Rick led that. I shouldn't say he did that. Rick led that with ideas. I'll tell you what, one of the most wonderful things about all of that is the people were so proud of themselves.

They had done it. He didn't do it. He didn't give them a bunch of orders. He didn't create a new three-inch binder with all the stuff that you put on a shelf.

He helped them to realize their potential. Their potential was there all along, but it wasn't liberated in a way that they could make continuous progress.

I must say, one of the great frustrations that was seen with this wonderful success was how hard it was to get the medical community at large, even after an article was written about this in a refereed journal, to get the medical profession in the United States to adopt these ideas on their own ground in their own terms. This led me to say, "There's something really strange about this, working in this medical community. It's hard to get perfect ideas through the wallboard."

It's frustrating.

Habitual Excellence

Anyway, I want to go back up to the top and just share a few ideas with you that, hopefully, will have some carrying power for you. Rick mentioned the term that, for me, is an umbrella.

It's a term of "habitual excellence."

I pause because habitual excellence to me means *everything*. One of the things I discovered, in the different privileged responsibilities I've had, is that it's not possible for an organization to be *partially* habitually excellent. There's a tendency to regress toward the mean.

One of the frustrations in health and medical care across the country — I'm all over the country and have been now for the better part of two decades talking about these things — is that people are inclined to do projects. It's amazing how much progress you can make with a project for a period of time.

It's also amazing how there's an erosion of success if you're surrounded by stuff that's not habitually excellent. It's really hard to protect an excellent experience if your interfaces are with parts of the organization that aren't excellent, because they pull you down.

> ***I believe organizations are either***
> ***habitually excellent or they're not.***

You can't be partially habitually excellent. You need to strive for the whole thing. I have to tell you, I didn't get a lightning bolt. I've been on a lifelong learning journey. Maybe I'll tell you a little war story about foundational things.

Leading at Alcoa

In March of 1987, I had been on the board of Alcoa for a year. I was then the president of the International Paper Company. The outside board members came to me, the other ones, and said, "We want you to come to Alcoa and be the chairman, the CEO of Alcoa."

I went home and talked to my wife about it. We were living in Connecticut. I worked in Midtown, Manhattan. When I told her, "I really think I ought to go do this thing in Pittsburgh," she was not sure that was a good idea.

[laughter]

She'd never been to Pittsburgh. Like most of you, she had this idea about, "Oh my God, we're going to this God-forsaken place. I love Connecticut." It was nice and the kids were there. We decided we would go. Nancy and I will be married, in September, 59 years. We've been at this a while.

[laughter]

[applause]

I had three months from the time I decided I was going to go to Alcoa until I went. I went to New York and met with a financial analyst who covered Alcoa to find out what they thought. What kind of organization is this? What do you think their prospects are? I went to Boeing, because they were a big customer, to find out "what kind of a supplier is Alcoa?"

I went to Anheuser-Busch because Alcoa made all of the aluminum can sheet for Coke and Pepsi and beer. I went and visited some plants. As a board member, I'd visited a little bit. I wanted to see more. I wanted to have an understanding of "what kind of a place is this?" Along with that, I had over the years worked in a bunch of different settings Rick didn't mention.

Early in my life, I worked as a construction engineer in Alaska supervising the building of communication sites all over the state. Most of you are not old enough to remember this. When we still had the Iron Curtain, we were building missile detection systems in Alaska to protect us from missile launches from Russia. I was a construction engineer building these sites. I did that.

I went to school. I did the Veterans' Administration, and the Office of Management and Budget, and International Paper. Along the way, I had an opportunity to witness a whole lot of different work environments, and ways that people worked and

A Playbook for Habitual Excellence

related to each other, and different ways that people who were in leadership positions led.

Along the way, I saw a whole lot of things that I liked and I saw a whole lot of things that I silently swore to myself that if I'm ever privileged to be in charge, I'm sure as hell not going to do that. I had a long list of, this is what it ought to be like.

After three months of introspection and talking to people outside of Alcoa, I took out an 8.5 x 11 piece of blue-lined tablet paper and wrote down my agenda. At the top of my agenda, I wrote "safety."

There were a lot of other things like:

> *"become the best in the world at everything we do,"*

and expressions of

> *"get rid of things that are in the way,"*

and

> *"seek to be the principal company in this industry everywhere in the world, not just in the United States and Canada but everywhere in the world."*

Nobody Should Get Hurt at Work

At the top of my list was safety. I tell you why safety was at the top of my list.

One of the things I had discovered working with a lot of different organizations, every organization of any size that I've ever had anything to do with... I'll bet it's true here. There's an annual report. It says in the annual report, "Our people are our most important resource."

It's almost like it's an obligation for people who sign their name at the bottom to say, "Our people really matter a lot. They're our most important resource." I would say, in most places, it's not true.

> ***If it were true [that people are our most important resource], people would not be hurt at work.***

If it's your most important resource, why wouldn't you organize yourself in such a way that the people who are supposed to be your most important resource, are never hurt at work?

On June the 15th of 1987, the lost-workday rate at Alcoa was 1.87. For some of you, I have to calibrate what that means. The way we keep data about injuries to workers is the rate per 100 workers. In the United States in June of 1987, the lost-workday rate for every industry in the United States was five, which means five out of every 100 people who worked in the United States had an injury at work that caused them to miss at least one day of work.

In June of 1987, Alcoa thought they were really good at what they did. The first day I was there, I asked Charlie DiMascio, who was the vice president for safety, to come and bring all of his facts with him so that we could talk about safety. Charlie was delighted to be there on my first day in the building. He was proud of what the facts were.

After he shared it all with me, I said,

> **"You know, Charlie, this is really great but I don't want to blindside you but I want you to know that I am going to say from this day forward that if you work at Alcoa, you should never be hurt at work."**

That was a stretch even for Charlie, for me to be going around saying, "We're going to have an injury-free workplace."

I explained to him the reasoning. If our people are really important, why wouldn't we organize ourselves in such a way that people never get hurt at work? It was necessary to clear out a lot of underbrush. It still exists, a lot of places all over the world, a notion of occupational hazard. If you work here, there are some things that could injure you. You should understand that there are those risks. We don't want you to be hurt but it's inevitable.

From "Accidents" to "Incidents"

It was necessary to change the language. Still, at a lot of places, people talk about accidents. If you think about it, the phrase that goes with accidents is, "We couldn't help it. God must have intended us to be hurt. Nobody wanted it. Nobody planned it. Nobody intended it but we have accidents."

I said, "No, no. We're not going to have any accidents at Alcoa. We're going to have incidents." The word "incidents" gives you intellectual permission to figure out what went wrong. How can we make sure it never happens again anywhere?

Visiting Sites and Making a Commitment

I went out and every place I went, I talked about the injury-free workplace. I went to our big plant in Tennessee. I'll tell you how big it was. It was so big that the town where we were was called Alcoa, Tennessee, outside of Knoxville.

There are 4,000 people there, huge rolling machines, a gigantic plant. I went down, much like I did yesterday afternoon [here at UVA]. I was privileged to spend half a day visiting some of your workplaces and talking with people about what's going on, which was great.

I spent the morning walking through the plant, talking to people, asking them about their families, and how long have you been here, and tell me more about the work, the child-like questions. "Tell me more. Why are you doing that?" Really interesting. Then we had lunch.

At lunch, we were 75 people. Half of them were from the supervisory ranks and the other half were from the organized workforce. In those days, Alcoa had the Aluminum Workers Union, and the Steelworkers Union, and the Auto Workers Union, and the International Machinery Workers Union.

In 1987, even though none of them were old enough to have been there, they remembered what it was like in 1935 when the company called in the Pinkerton private security workforce and shot some of the employees because they were having a dispute. When I got there in July of 1987, it was like the shooting happened yesterday.

That was the antipathy between the people who did the work and the so-called supervisors. Here I have these 75 people. They said, "Do you want to talk? Do you want to say something?" I thought I did. I stood up and I said, "You know, most organizations I've ever been part of have what I call a tom-tom network. It is really efficient.

"You can't figure out how it works but important messages have a way of being everywhere and everybody has a take on it. So, I hope the tom-tom network works in Alcoa and you all know that I have said people who work here should never be hurt at work." People start looking down. The tom-tom network had worked. They all largely didn't believe it.

I said, "I want you to know I really mean it. So, to those in the supervisory workforce, this is what I want to say. I do mean it and we in Alcoa are never going to budget for safety again.

We're not going to budget for safety.

"As soon as anyone in this place identifies a risk that could cause someone to be hurt, I want you to fix it. And, for you supervisors, don't worry about it. I will figure out how to pay for it." My friend Ernie Edwards who's here who was a controller of Alcoa at the time, he and his colleagues practically died.

They thought I was unleashing this unmanageable thing where people were going to put up all kinds of frivolous stuff to spend money on it in the name of safety because the chairman said, "Don't budget for safety," which means it's a free pass. I, honestly, was not worried about that. I turned out to be right.

Then I said to the hourly workers, "You heard what I said to them. So, here's what I want to say to you, 412-555-1234, that's my home phone number."[4] Not many Fortune 50 CEOs were giving out their personal home phone number to hourly workers in Tennessee.

I did it because I wanted them to know and said to them, "If the supervisors don't do what I just said to you, I want you to call me." I went out of my way. We ended up with 343 plants in 43 countries. I had to go to a lot of different places. I was on my travel schedule. About three weeks later, I was home at night, about 11 o'clock, and the phone rang.

The Phone Rings

I picked up the phone wondering, "What could this be at 11 o'clock at night?" The voice on the other end said, "This is Tony from Tennessee. You were down here and said all this hot stuff about three weeks ago about safety. Well, I'm calling to tell you for the last three days we had this roller conveyor system where we take ingots out of the casting pit that weigh 600 pounds.

"We roll them over this roller conveyor to the rolling mill where we mount them up in the mill and then we roll these ingots into can sheet. For the last three days, we've had a section of the roller conveyor that's broken. So, a bunch of us have to get together.

"It takes a lot of us to lift this ingot off the working conveyer, over the broken conveyer to the next working conveyer and we're

4 His actual phone number has been changed for this text, but he gave out his real number to workers.

worried about hurting our backs. If we drop this on our feet, we'd crush our feet. So, we want to know, what is all this stuff you said about safety? It's sure not real here."

I said, "Tony, thank you. I will call you back in a little while."

I called the Alcoa switchboard - in those days we had an operator on duty 24 hours a day - and got the telephone number of the plant manager in Tennessee. I called him up and woke him up out of a dead sleep and said to him, "I just had a call from Tony at your plant. He tells me about this broken conveyer. I want you to go down to the plant and after you get the conveyor fixed, I want you to call me back."

I waited and waited. About four o'clock in the morning, the phone rang. It was the plant manager. He said, "We fixed the conveyer and I'm sorry they had to call you."

I said, "Good. I'm glad you got it fixed. I don't ever want to get this kind of a call again."

Word Spreads Quickly

Then it was interesting. The Alcoa tom-tom network went into overdrive.

[laughter]

I didn't have to go to 343 locations because people said, "He may be crazy, but he really means this, and we need to turn, too. We need to go after potential injuries." It was the beginning of coalescing the people around, for me, a really important part of habitual excellence. In order to have a workplace where people never get hurt at work, you have to identify every risk.

If there is an incident, you need to be on it immediately. You need to do a root-cause analysis. Then the power of large organizations, once you've done that, if you have absolute transparency and complete information sharing, you don't have to learn the same lesson over, and over, and over again.

That's how you leverage an organization:

By learning from everything gone wrong and sharing it across all of the artificial boundaries that we've created with organizational designs so that everyone is a beneficiary of learning.

Information Belongs to Everybody

One of my basic beliefs is, in a really great organization, the information belongs to everybody in the organization.

I had a rule that said, everything we have belongs to every employee except for information that, inadvertently released, could cause somebody to go to jail. In the aluminum business and at big companies, that means you dare not have, in-between quarterly reporting periods, financial information released because people can use it to speculate and gain an advantage in the market.

A Real-Time Safety System

Everything else, I wanted everybody to have. One of the things we did early on was to create the Alcoa real-time safety data system with this idea. It was interesting. I have a sense that you have some of this pace going on in your own organization now.

I said to these two young women who had recently graduated from Carnegie Mellon, "I want to create a real-time safety data system so that all of our locations in the world can hook up to the Internet every morning and post on a real-time basis every near-miss, every OSHA recordable, every lost-workday case, every incident beginning with the name of the person."

My lawyers hated that. My lawyers said, "Oh, my God! You're going to equip the tort bar and sue our socks off by having this information out there on the Internet when we have somebody injured and we identify them by name."

I'll tell you why I wanted to do it by name. It's the same as the 1,000 line days thing. I wanted it to be human. I didn't want it to be about numbers. I wanted the name so people would say, "Oh, my God! I know Mary. I know Mary."

The first field in the data that went on the Internet every day, the name of the person, the circumstances of the injury, when possible, the root-cause analysis with an expectation that within 24 hours after the information was posted, including with the root-cause analysis, every one of the people in 343 locations would adopt a new practice so we didn't have to learn over, and over, and over again.

***I wanted it to be human. I didn't
want it to be about numbers.***

It was unbelievable how powerful it was. In 13 years, I was there for 13 years, and we never had a lawsuit that was based on our real-time safety data system, not a single one.

Like a Magnet Toward Zero

We got better, and better, and better. Importantly, this was not a straight line. Really important process improvements can't be dictated to go from here to here. You don't go to zero overnight. There's a learning process.

We began to see rates of improvement of like 30 percent, sometimes 50 percent, on an ever-smaller number. Here's another thing. A lot of stuff we learn isn't true. You all know about the law of diminishing returns. You often hear it about, "We can't afford to get the last part of pollution out because it costs so much more money to get it out."

I tell you what, the law of diminishing returns is bull-something. It's amazing when you get really good at what you do, there's an acceleration effect so that your rate of improvement increases when you get close to zero, it's almost like there's a magnet on zero the better you get. It's in everything. It's not just about workplace safety. It is amazing.

I, honestly, didn't look this morning. I've got my phone. I could do it right this minute. If you go on the Internet, and look at the Alcoa site, and click on the safety box, you'll see the lost-workday rate year-to-date at Alcoa, where I've been gone now for 14 years. The lost-workday rate is 0.072.

The People Own Their Safety

Now, I'll tell you what's really great about that. I love it so much because it says, "It's not about me. The people own their own safety. They have not forgotten, and they've passed it on to a new generation of people and it is foundational for what they do now." I believe these ideas apply to all kinds of process improvement.

If you can identify things gone wrong in real-time and solve them in something like real-time, and share the learning, you can lever an organization so that it can achieve amazing things.

It's really interesting to me. Yesterday afternoon, I was privileged to go and visit a number of organizational elements here. I loved what I saw in the PICU.

The people in the PICU, I don't know how many of you know, it is fantastic what they have done. They have largely used these ideas to take your pediatric intensive care unit to a place that's commendable. It's not at zero yet but, boy, they are really good at what they do. This is not a set of foreign ideas to use. You're already practicing in some elements.

It demonstrates right here the power of shared learning and a sense of we did it together.

The Power of Theoretical Limits

I'm going to give you a few more ideas. One idea that I've found of great utility, beginning when I was in the Executive Office of the President at the Bureau of the Budget, which turned into OMB, is an idea that I call the concept of a theoretical limit.

When I was there, in an executive office, we had all these unbelievable issues and problems. I found there was great value in saying to myself when someone was proposing that we start a new program or activity,

"If it were perfect, what would it look like?"
For me, the theoretical limit is perfect. It's an idea
that applies to everything.

If you ask yourself, "What's the theoretical limit for injuries to workers?" the answer is zero. What's the theoretical limit for hospital-acquired infections? It's zero. That's the theoretical limit.

One of the things that I found really useful about this concept of a theoretical limit is it's not used to bludgeon people.

It's used to set up an intellectual construct so that you can take a measurement of where you are and compare it to what perfect looks like. It drains the swamp so you can see stuff that you couldn't easily see otherwise. I gave you the Allegheny General stuff and the two percent thing. Two percent, how many places are 98 percent good?

You can take a lot of conceit out of, "Hey, we're 98 percent perfect." What about the 19 people who died? That's a different way to think about it. The theoretical limit, you say to yourself, "What about the 19 people who died?" They don't want to do that. It unleashes your intellectual ability to recalibrate how you think about what you're doing.

The Things Only a Leader Can Do

I like, as an intellectual discipline, the idea of a theoretical limit. I also want to share a couple of other ideas with you. I said to you I believe organizations are either habitually excellent or they're not. There are some things that I believe only a leader can do.

There are some things you can't do from the bottom of the organization. As much as you may want to do it, you cannot create the fundamentals for habitual excellence from the bottom of the organization. It's the leaders' responsibility to create the cultural conditions in an organization where people can answer yes to three questions every day.

Three Questions

This is not a lightning bolt. This is decades of experience, of learning, working in organizations. An organization has a potential for habitual excellence, people can say yes to three questions every day.

Here are the three questions.

1) **Are you treated with dignity and respect every day by everyone you encounter without regard to race, or gender, or nationality, or pay level, or rank, or any other qualifying characteristic?**

Everyone can say, "I'm treated with dignity and respect every day," in the same measure without any hesitation. I have to tell you there are not many organizations that I know of where people can honestly say yes to that. In health medical care, there is a tendency toward hierarchy.

I would warrant this to you. The people who clean the rooms are as important as the people who do the surgery. If they don't do their work well, a perfect surgery gets undone. Are those people important? Yeah.

I had this mantra at Alcoa. If you're here, you're important. If you're not important, you shouldn't be here. We just haven't figured it out yet.

Everybody should be treated with the same dignity and respect no matter what you do. What you do here is really important. I'm going to link it for you. I'm going to take you back to the Tennessee plant. One of the things I observed in the Tennessee plant is there were oil leaks on the floor.

There were people who were hired and spent 20, 30 years sweeping sawdust on oil leaks on the plant floor. Were they important? Absolutely. They were keeping people from being hurt, from slipping and falling. After I'd been there a little while, I said, "You know, this is not really a good idea. How about if we had forklift trucks that didn't leak?"

[laughter]

Our people said, "Oh, my God! Well, God intended them to leak," or something.

[laughter]

I went to Komatsu in Japan and said to them, "I want forklift trucks that don't leak." Pretty soon, they started producing forklift trucks that didn't leak. We could take those people who were pushing sawdust and get them to do something that added value instead of spent important human resources of materials to, in effect, do repair work.

They were busy as heck. They weren't just standing around. They were doing work, but it was work that was driven by a failure. It was a process failure. It was an equipment failure. It was because we didn't ask that child-like question, why do forklift trucks have to leak? They don't. They don't.

It wasn't that the people were bad. They were doing the best they could, dealing with a problem that costs money without value. An important part of dignity and respect is being constantly on alert for, how can we eliminate activity that doesn't add value so that we can give dignity and respect to the people who are doing the work? That's giving people respect.

Here's my second question. Most people can't get by number one. Number two is this:

2) **Can people say, "I'm given the things I need, education, and training, and financial support, and encouragement — that's really important — so that I can make a contribution to this organization that gives meaning to my life"?**

The last part of that is really important. If you stop with making a contribution to the organization, it's about extracting something from people.

In a really great organization, people get meaning in their life from the work that they do because it is so rewarding. They understand why they're important.

Let me go back to the people who clean the rooms.

If they don't have meaning in their life, it's a failure of leadership explaining to them and to everyone else, "You are really important and let me tell you why. You could undo the surgery if you don't do your job with perfection every day and, therefore, you are important, and you should take pride in every successful surgery without a hospital-acquired infection."

No matter how menial you may think the work is, if it's truly important it should give meaning to the life of the people who do it. They should be able to say yes to number two.

Number three, then, shouldn't be too hard.

3) **Are you recognized every day by someone whose judgment you value?**

I don't mean claps in the cafeteria.

I mean as you're going off the ward at night, somebody you care about says to you, "Great job today." The recognition thing is so important to have an organization where people are together. It doesn't have to be from Rick. People will take a nice thank you on the way out at night and it will give them that complete circle of, "This place gives meaning in my life."

Leaders Have to Constantly Work at It

That can only happen if the leader decides that's how life is going to be in the organization. I have to tell you, in the 13 years I was at Alcoa, I worked hard on this aspect of creating a place where people were together.

I would say with 143,000 people, maybe 85 percent or 90 percent were with it. It's never over. You can't just ordain it and say, "This is the way it's going to be."

Constantly work at it. You have to constantly look for things that counter your message.

I'll give you a few examples of things that counter your message. I was into saying people are really important and believing it. Discovering we did things by habit that have been around for a long time, that made a lie out of the idea that everybody is equally important, that we need everybody.

When I first went to Alcoa, there was a coffee shop on the ground floor. At 5:30 on the first morning, I was there. I went into the coffee shop. Lucy was there. I got to know it was Lucy. I got my coffee, and a wheat toast, and a grapefruit juice, and read my paper.

When I went in on the second morning, there were two executive vice presidents sitting at the counter. I said to them, "I'll bet you've never been here at 5:30 before and you shouldn't be here today because the fact that I'm here doesn't mean you need to be here. This is my private reading time."

[laughter]

I think they were relieved. It wasn't their habit to get to work at 5:30. I'm not saying everybody should get to work at 5:30. It was my habit of working full-time and going to graduate school and all that stuff. I became like a doctor in training or something where I didn't know there was a clock anymore. I didn't expect everybody to do that.

Do We Do That for All the People?

Somebody said to me, "Well, you know, you really don't have to go to that coffee shop and talk to Lucy who's smoking behind the counter." This was a while ago. "Up on the top floor just right above your office where the corporate boardroom is, every morning the people set up coffee, and pastries, and fruit, and things for the executives. So, you can go up there and get your coffee."

I said, "That's really great. Do we do that for all the people in the smelters? Do all the hourly workers get coffee, and pastries, and fruit when they come to work?" No. I said, "What are we doing spending the shareholders' money on a perk for executives? What the hell is that about?"

I said, "It's OK with me if it's up there and if it's convenient and all that but the people who use it should pay for it."

It was the beginning of a journey of discovery of stuff that basically said, "The message isn't really true." The old saw about rank has its privileges, I believe, it's completely wrong.

> **Rank should have its responsibilities, which are heavy, and demanding, and all of that. It's not about when you move up in the organization, you get more privileges.**

I did crazy things like saying to people, "Doesn't it seem right to you that the people who get here first should be able to park closest to the building? What are those lined-off places with names on them that tell people, 'Don't park here because there's somebody more important than you'?" I said, "That doesn't seem right to me."

I systematically worked on eliminating all of the symbols and signs that said to people, "We're not all the same. We're not on an equal footing." It took a while to get the rhythm of that in the organization so that people understood. I'll tell you one. It's back to the Tennessee example.

After I'd been there a short time, they said to me, "Well, you should know we have this lodge in Tennessee and it can sleep 25 people. It's a beautiful log structure that was built a long time ago." It turned out there were 25 employees who were on the plant payroll who didn't do anything but work at Alcoa's Boar's Head Inn.

There was an 18-hole championship golf course, and an English bowling green, and a stocked pond where you could catch fish this big, and 160 acres planted in corn so they could attract quail and go down there and shoot quail.

Before I got there, the chairman got on a plane early on Friday afternoon with his family and flew down to Scona in Tennessee to spend the weekend.

It was also used for customer entertainment. It seemed, to me, an artifact of the past when the ownership of the place were families. When it became a public company, I said to myself, "What are we doing?"

There were 25 people supporting this luxury for the executives to go and enjoy themselves on a weekend, flying the company plane which costs $4,000 an hour to put in the air. One of the things I did after I'd been there a while...this was not a popular move...

[laughter]

I gave Scona to the Nature Conservancy. People thought that was crazy. I bulldozed the lodge to make sure it never came back. I wanted to make the point that we should not be affording ourselves luxurious living. It sent the wrong message to everybody about what kind of organization this is.

Some of the things I did were really economically beneficial. I discovered we owned three apartments in the Essex House on Central Park South. Do you know what they were for? Executives went to New York with their families to see Broadway shows on the weekend and charged it to the company. I sold the apartments. Made a hell of a lot of money.

[laughter]

One Important Accomplishment at Alcoa

It is really important, as you're on a journey to being habitually excellent, to work on identifying things that defeat the message of habitual excellence, and everyone matters, and we're in this together.

> *I accomplished one important thing at Alcoa. I got more than 100,000 people to ask child-like questions and gave them the power to change.*

Things that didn't make sense didn't have to go up the hierarchy. They had the power to change.

Making Perfect Product with No Waste

One more concept that may be useful to you, the standard that we should have for what we're doing where we're making things...This is in some ways easier than the work that you do. Where we're making products, here's the standard.

24 hours a day, we should make perfect product that goes to the customer and does what we said it would do, 24 hours a day. 24 hours a day means you get perfect utilization of your capital

equipment, and the human beings, and the energy you consume. There's no waste. There's no repair work. There's no downtime.

It's out there, the theoretical limit. When I started going around the plants and saying this concept of 24 hours a day and said to people, "Where do you think you are on the curve of 24 hours?"

They said, "98 percent."

I said, "Wow! That's really terrific. I spend a lot of time in plants around the world and not many plants are really at 98 percent. Let's test this proposition a little bit."

I'd say, "Do you ever have equipment that breaks down and causes you not to be able to make product?"

"Oh, yeah."

I said, "Well, that's interesting. How could you possibly be at 98 percent?" They said, "Well, we don't count that time."

[laughter]

"Say, that's really interesting. So, do you do preventive maintenance here?"

"Oh, yeah. We do. On Friday afternoon — this is in Warrick, Indiana — we close the plant at four o'clock. Turn everything off. From four o'clock until midnight, we do preventive maintenance on everything. We fix everything. We oil things. We change out equipment, there are bearings that are worn out and stuff like that."

I said, "That's really great. I would like to know one more thing. During that period, when you're doing preventive maintenance, what's the longest elapsed time that you're actually doing an individual task, like changing out filters or changing out a bearing or something?" The answer is 36 minutes.

If you can imagine, if you've got the people who are doing the work to do the preventive maintenance and the longest elapsed time is 36 minutes, to be generous if you only used an hour for preventive maintenance instead of eight hours for preventive maintenance, which was the standard, you in effect give yourself back seven hours worth of additional production capacity without spending a penny, just with an idea.

It's about ideas. It's not about some magic bullet. It's about ideas that make your work more satisfying, productive, and value-added.

So Much Opportunity in Healthcare

One of the big things I noticed when I traveled around health medical care systems in the country is the amount of hunting and fetching people are doing, looking for things that aren't where they're supposed to be.

I said yesterday we've been places where there's a shortage of materials, where there are the push-up ceilings that are closer, people put the things they don't think are going to be available when they need them up in the ceiling.

Then they put themselves at risk. They get on a little step stool to get up there to get their stuff, to recover their stuff, or the IV pump is in your locker or something. People are pressuring the purchasing department. We need more of this and that.

If you put it all in one big pile, it's twice as much as you really need if it were where it was supposed to be, when it's supposed to be there, sterilized and ready for use. There is so much opportunity.

From Cost-Cutting to Value Improvement

Another really important idea is that getting more excellent is not, in my judgment, about cost-cutting. It's about value improvement, which is not the same thing as cost-cutting.

If you can imagine eliminating hunting, fetching, and other non-value-added things and think about applying that same time to patient care and the things you would like to do if only you can really create a transformed institution where almost everything you do is adding value.

One thing related to that, in the 13 years I was at Alcoa, we improved our market value by 800 percent, with ideas.

We were not about cost-cutting.

We were about the 24-hour concept, being perfect at everything we do, and inventing new products for people.

My notion was dedication. People who work here, we the leadership, have an obligation to cause the organization to function in such a way that people are not fearful about their jobs and about the future, because...

it's really hard if you feel under the gun to be involved in continuous learning and continuous improvement.

Thank you all very much.

Questions for Reflection and Discussion

1. What "third grader" questions would you ask frontline employees the next time you are in the workplace?

2. "Safety" was the top goal on Paul's list as he prepared to become Alcoa's CEO. What would be the top goal on your list if you were preparing to become the CEO of a new organization? How you would expect an organization to react if you came in as its new CEO and stated safety as the goal? How would your current organization react to this?

3. Why did Paul give his home phone number to the workers at the plant in Tennessee? What message did that send? With current-day technology in mind, what equivalent action would you be willing to take?

4. What are the benefits of reporting safety data in "real time?" How does your organization currently define real time? What concrete steps can you take to close any gap between your organization's definition and what it should be?

Lean Healthcare Transformation Summit 2013

Introduction by Helen Zak, senior advisor for Value Capture, former president of Catalysis:

Paul was one of our first directors on the board at Catalysis. I got to know Paul well during our board meetings as well as the "Enduring Excellence" program for executives that Catalysis supported. I relentlessly encouraged Paul to share his wisdom in both a book and at our annual Lean Healthcare Transformation Summit. It took a couple of tries, but Paul agreed to share his thinking and wisdom with Healthcare Value Network members at the Summit, but I wasn't successful in getting him to do the book, unfortunately. I'm hoping that this ebook will be the proxy to inspire leaders, just as Paul did back in 2013 with his talk.

Helen Zak: Join me in welcoming Paul O'Neill. I've been asking him for almost two years now, could he come and speak to us, and share his words of wisdom.

Paul's had another rich career as a change agent, which has included being CEO of Alcoa and Treasury Secretary. That must have been a really interesting job. I hope you tell us a little bit about that.

Join me in welcoming Paul O'Neill.

[applause]

Paul O'Neill: Thank you, Helen. This has been a really pleasurable day for me because I was able to listen instead of talk. I listened to some really smart people talk about their own journey, and what they're doing, and their experience, and their dedication and passion to something I believe in pretty deeply.

The sessions I enjoyed today featured presenters asking questions. I thought, "Wow, that's really fun." I tend to be didactic which is not a good thing all the time. I thought I'd begin with a question.

Of all the people that are here today, how many of you are from an organization that has an annual report? Almost everybody knows about annual reports. How many of you will find in your annual report a statement that says, "Our people are our most important asset?" Does anybody have that?

Pretty much everyone. Let me ask you another question. How many of you work in an organization where 24 hours a day, you can go on the Internet, and you can see the OSHA recordable rate for your organization 24 hours a day, real time, and the lost workday injury rate for the people who work in your organization? A few people over here. I don't see many hands over here.

Let me tell you what I believe. I believe organizations are either habitually excellent, or they're not.

I believe, a way to demonstrate that an organization is truly on a journey toward, what I like to say, a goal that should go under the name of your institution, on the top of the stationery.

A statement that says, "Our goal is to be the best in the world at everything we do."

Then for me, the subtext is if that's what you aspire to, you aspire to be habitually excellent, best in the world at everything you do, wouldn't it be a pretty good idea to start with caring, really caring about the people who work in your institution?

All those institutions who say, their people are their most important resource or asset, I would say, "Show me the evidence." For me, the evidence begins with what has been demonstrated as possible.

Huge worldwide organizations, with injury rates in forbidding environments and cultures, where people are never hurt at work.

Not lower than last year. Not better than the industry average.

The Most Dangerous Industry in the U.S.

I wonder again, how many of you know that health and medical care, by the OSHA numbers, is the most dangerous industry in the United States?

The OSHA recordable rates in health and medical care across the country are five people out of every 100 who work in health medical care in a year's time in the United States have an OSHA recordable injury. The lost workday cases mean something more serious than a first aid case or something that required treatment in the office medical center. A lost workday case means, "I couldn't come to work today."

In my career, I've cared most about lost workday rates, because it's hard to fudge. You can non-report needlesticks or back strains that cause you to be assigned to the nursing station because you can't move around the floor. It's really hard to fake that you didn't show up today.

The lost workday rate across American medical care is something close to three out of every 100 people who have an injury at work, often serious enough that it causes them to miss at least one day of work.

Ten minutes ago, before I came up on stage, I got the Alcoa data up on my iPad, which is there 24 hours a day. It's recorded Greenwich Mean Time. The most recent report I found was 18:00 Greenwich Mean Time, which means a few hours ago the lost workday rate at Alcoa year to date, across the world, 0.065.

[applause]

Thank you for the applause, but you should know I've been out of there for 13 years.

[laughter]

I tell you what, I love the fact that the culture owns workplace safety. A lot of the people who work in that enterprise today, I'm a historical figure. If I'm in their mind at all, but the people in the organization own each other's welfare.

Now, why do I care about workplace safety?
It's obviously, morally, and ethically important
on its own bottom.

Let me go back to what I said at the beginning. I believe organizations are either habitually excellent or they're not. I believe, as much as we may be able to make headway in things like central line infections, and exposure to blood and body fluids, splashes, and the like.

I'm not going to believe we're serious in health and medical care about perfect patient care or about practicing Lean in a vigorous, energetic way every day until every organization that's represented here, in fact, *all* caregiving institutions across the United States can say, "We have on our website, real time information about the injuries that occur to the people that we say we care about."

That information is not for the purpose of blaming or shaming, but so that we can put into motion the ideas of Lean, and continuous learning, and continuous improvement. Until we are dedicated to the proposition that every injury is one we care about, and act on, and figure out how to eliminate the associated causes that produce an injury, I'm not going to believe we're serious.

It's great to have conferences, it's great to talk about the tools and techniques, of which I'm a great fan. I have a Shingo Prize. I have the Juran Medal from the American Society for Quality. I've been elected to the Manufacturing Hall of Fame at IndustryWeek.

I have all those tickets. I'll tell you what. I'll trade them all in, for a country where we demonstrated we cared about the people who work in our institutions, beginning with health and medical care. Hell, I may come back next year, so I can ask the question again. [laughs] Hopefully, get everyone to say, "Yes."

The Power of Habit

I'll tell you a few war stories to illustrate the point. As some of you know this, from Charles Duhigg's book about the *Power of Habit*, which he interviewed me for, and I didn't really know what he was going to do with it.

He captured a lot of really important ideas, but I don't think he captured, at least not as vibrantly as I would have wished, the connection between workplace safety and everything else.

I started on the day I went to Alcoa, on June 15th, 1987, by rolling in there after I'd been on the board for a year and got recruited from the other outside directors to come and become the chairman and CEO. I had three months between the time I was recruited and when I actually had to go.

I spent a lot of that time learning. I went to visit Anheuser-Busch and Boeing, big consumers of Alcoa's products. I went to visit suppliers. I went to visit the top-rated analyst in New York, who followed the company on a regular basis. I figured I could learn some things from them.

After three months, I sat down with an 8.5-by-11 blue-lined sheet of tablet paper to answer this question — when you leave Alcoa, what do you want to be remembered for?

At the top of my page, I wrote "safety" with this idea in mind -- that I was going to go and on the first day I was going to announce to the safety director and then through the organization,

> *"From this day forward, it shall be Alcoa's goal to assure that people who work here are never hurt at work."*

I have to give you some facts to set the background for this situation. In June of 1987, the lost workday injury rate across American industry - it's come down some now - across American industry, five out of 100 people who were employed in the United States had an injury at work that caused them to miss at least one day of work.

The Alcoa number June 15th of 1987 was 1.86. They were really proud of where they were because the environment they worked in has metal flowing at 2,000 degrees and lots of clanking overhead cranes lifting heavy metal and carrying it across plant floors, and plant trucks racing around on the floors with unmarked aisles and all the rest of that. They were really proud.

When I told Charlie DiMascio, who was vice president for safety, "Charlie, from now on, our goal is zero," even Charlie was taken aback because he didn't imagine it could be better than 1.86.

Behind my back, not to my face, people who'd been there a long time said, "He doesn't know anything about making aluminum.

He doesn't know anything about our industry, except what he maybe scraped up in a few board meetings and talking to people for the last three months.

"As soon as we have a next price cycle and our earnings go in the tank, he'll shut up about this. We can go on being as good as we are, which is impossible to improve on and we can get on with our business." I knew that would happen.

It was not a surprise to me that people would say, "We're as good as we can possibly be."

It's interesting that across industries - forest products, chemicals, aluminum, auto parts, auto manufacturers, health and medical care - the excuses are all the same.

"We can't afford to be better than we are. If we're going to be better, we're going to have to have more people working on this subject."

From Accidents to Incidents

Latently, mostly, people believe God intended for us to be hurt. Accidents are inevitable, they think.

Think about the word "accident." It has the weight of inevitability.

When I was at Alcoa, I set out to change the language and convince people, we were not ever going to have an accident again. We were going to have incidents - because if we had an incident, the human brain could work on figuring out how not to have that incident again.

If you believe accidents are inevitable, believe me, you're never going to get rid of central line infections. I know this is an ongoing conversation in organizations. The interesting thing about our culture as a general matter - it's not everybody, but as a general matter, we don't like to set goals we don't think we can achieve.

One of the pushbacks I got at Alcoa was people said, "We don't want to set a zero goal because we don't really believe we can achieve it."

I said, "Great."

I took leadership with me out on the plant floor and talked to 40 or 50 people in the plant environment, and said to them, "You know what? I've said we should have zero injuries — incidents — through our workforce. Some of your leaders who have a lot more experience than I do don't believe we should set a zero goal because we don't think we can achieve it.

> *"I'd like to do this. If you want to make sure, if we're going to have a goal that is a positive number, raise your hand if you want to make sure we reach our goal."*

There were no volunteers for people who wanted to be hurt.

I said, "Why do we have to have a positive goal? Why is a little bit better than last year, or 30 percent better than last year, OK? It's not OK. We may not be able to get to zero in a year," and we didn't.

We did not get to zero in a year, but we began improving at a rate of 30 to 50 percent a year over 13 years.

We got really down there in the less than single digits in the 13 years I was there.

I told you the number today is 0.065. That's ownership of a set of ideas that begin with really doing something to make good on the proposition that our people are our most important asset.

Real Leadership and Three Questions

I don't think any of these things, including the safety goal, can happen without what I call "real leadership."

I have a lament. I don't think we do a decent job in our education process of causing people to think deeply and individually about what leadership means.

For me, it's not just the person that gets paid the most money. It's not that. It's not an organizational position.

Leadership is about a specific set of things, including creating a culture, a culture, where the three questions John [Toussaint, M.D] shared with you this morning, people can say yes to every day.

I want to remind you of those, and I want to elaborate a little bit. John gave you the headlines. I want to give you a little bit more than headlines to make sure you get the texture of these ideas. I don't believe these ideas can exist in an organization unless the leader articulates, owns, and practices the ideas that produce these cultural responses every day.

Here's again the first question:

Can every person in the organization say every day without any hesitation, "I'm treated with dignity and respect every day by everyone I encounter without regard to my rank, my pay level, my educational attainment, my gender, my ethnicity, my nationality, my race or any other qualifier that you want to put in front of it?"

Everyone can say every day without any reservation, "I am treated with dignity and respect every day by everyone I encounter." Let's put it in a health-and-medical care context.

Do the people who clean rooms get the same quotient of dignity and respect as a surgeon who produces 25 percent of the revenue? I don't personally know many organizations where that is literally true.

It cannot be true unless the leader is dedicated to that idea and sets in motion a continuous process of taking away anything and everything that interferes with the ability of every individual to say yes.

If the leader isn't dedicated to that proposition, if it's OK for people to be abusive out on the wards because, in other regards, they were good or useful or even a superior performer, forget it.

This is a rule without exceptions. It's not OK to make exceptions.

The second question is can people say yes to,

"Am I given the things I need - tools, equipment, education, training, encouragement - encouragement is important - so that I can make a contribution to this organization that gives meaning to my life?"

We're at this 8, 10, 12 hours a day.

If you don't get meaning in your life at work, you're probably going to have a pretty stilted less-than-could-be life. That's really criminal. Please notice: these first two things I said to you don't cost more money. They don't require a new department.

In fact, I'm fond of saying to illustrate the point, "If you show me an organization with a vice president for equal opportunity, I'll show you an organization that probably doesn't have equal opportunity." Show me an organization where quality is owned by the quality department. You can be pretty sure they don't have quality there.

If central cultural characteristics are assigned to a department, forget it.

The third question is if people can say yes, without any hesitation, to:

"Am I recognized for what I do every day by someone whose opinion I value?"

Recognition is not a blow-off ceremony in the cafeteria where the person who's giving the award can't even pronounce everybody's name.

That's not what I mean by recognition in this trilogy of necessary things that only a leader can establish in an organization. Again, you can't get to zero safety incidents with cheerleading. You can't get to these three propositions with cheerleading. This is not about writing it on the wall and believing as a leader that you've accomplished a purpose.

It needs to be in the organization. It needs to be owned by the people. For me, a reason to begin with workplace safety was because I believed it was a goal no one could argue with. It's related to another one of what I think are necessary duties of a real leader to articulate aspirational goals that are basically non-arguable.

Now that doesn't mean I think the leader has to get this flash of light from above to establish these aspirational goals. Ideally, the aspirational goals come out of a careful conversation or organization where people talk together about what our aspirational goals should be. I nominate workplace safety as an aspirational goal.

I found at Alcoa that people didn't believe that we could get to zero. A third thing that I think only a leader can do is take away excuses. Excuses are everywhere in every kind of industry. People have reasons why not.

One of the things a real leader needs to do is
take away excuses.

Activating the Tom-Tom Network

Three weeks after I'd been at Alcoa, I went to a gigantic plant in a place called Alcoa, Tennessee. It tells you something about how important they were in that community outside of Knoxville, 3,500 people. I'll tell you a little background setting for going to this plant. It was built in the middle 1930s. The Alcoa leadership was really quite visionary in the 1930s.

The leaders believed that we were at risk as a nation in getting into a major military conflict. In the middle '30s, if you can believe it, they spent a fortune during the Depression building this huge mill complex to smelt aluminum to roll it into sheet for aircraft applications six years before we desperately needed the material.

There's another aspect to this place in 1935 before they built the big rolling mill. There was a labor dispute. The management called in the Pinkertons. The Pinkertons shot a bunch of employees. When I went there for the first time, this was now August of 1987.

It was like the Pinkertons had been there yesterday if you looked at the relationship between the supervisory workforce and the people who did the work. It was still an atmosphere corroded by an experience that people don't forget. It was like it happened yesterday.

I spent the morning walking through the floor, talking with the people on the line, asking them about their families, how long they'd been there. What are the technical things that you have to manage here to make sure that you produce product that doesn't fall apart when we put it on an airplane? Then they had lunch. There were 75 people invited to lunch, half from the organized hourly ranks, and the other half in the supervisory group.

In those days Alcoa was organized by the US Steelworkers, the Aluminum Workers, the Machinists, one other that's slipping my mind. Anyway, four major unions represented the people who worked in that plant. At lunch they said after we had eaten, "Would you like to say something?" I said I would.

I got up and I said, "I assume that Alcoa has a tom-tom network." This was before we all had iPhones for those of you who are too young to understand the idea of tom-tom networks. In all of the organizations I've ever been a part of, including back to the days when I worked as a construction engineer in Alaska in the middle 1950s, there was a tom-tom network, especially for gossip.

You could be sure, if there was a piece of meaty gossip someplace in the organization, it was like wildfire. Everybody knew it. I believed in tom-tom networks.

I said to the people, "My guess is you've got a really active tom-tom network. If it's working as well as I think it probably does, you already know that I've said people who work at Alcoa should never be hurt at work.

"I mean it. I want to demonstrate to you I really mean it by saying this to all of you. Alcoa will never again budget for safety. As soon as anyone in one of our facilities recognizes the potential for the way we're equipped or organized that somebody could be hurt,

I want you to fix it right now. I will make it my personal responsibility to figure out how we're going to pay for it."

The financial people in the organization were terrified.

[laughter]

They could not believe the CEO was announcing, "We'll spend whatever we need to on safety." It was like taking away one of their major levers.

I said, "As soon as anybody identifies a thing, just fix it."

To the supervisory staff, I said, "That's your responsibility to make sure that happens."

To the hourly people, "I want to do this. I want to give you my home phone number."

I gave them 412-555-1234. Please don't write it down.

[laughter]

And I said to them, "If they don't do what I just said, you call me up. Call me up."

About three weeks later, about 11 o'clock at night, I got a phone call.

A voice on the other end said, "Well, I'm calling you from the Tennessee plant. You were down here a few weeks ago. You said all this hot stuff about we shouldn't be hurt at work and all the rest of that.

"I'm calling you to tell you for the last three days we've had a broken roller conveyor system to transport these 600-pound ingots from the casting pit to the rolling mill. It's a long roller conveyor maybe 300 feet long. There's a section that's been broken in that roller conveyor for the last three days.

"As a consequence, those of us in the workforce on the floor are lifting, a bunch of us, those 600-pound ingots, putting them on a dolly, taking them around the broken conveyor, putting them on the next section of working conveyor. We're going to hurt our backs. If we drop one of these things on our feet, we'd be permanently disabled.

"I'm calling up to tell you this isn't exactly what we thought you meant."

[laughter]

I said, "Thank you very much." I got on the phone and called the Alcoa central operator, which was there 24 hours a day, and said to her, "I need to have the phone number for the plant manager for the Alcoa, Tennessee plant." When she got me, I called him up, got him out of bed, and told him the story.

I said to him, "I want you to go down to the plant. I want you to get that conveyor fixed. I want you to call me when it's fixed and I don't ever want to get another call."

At about four o'clock in the morning, he called and told me the conveyor had been fixed. Then the Alcoa tom-tom network really went into business.

[laughter]

Safety for Everybody

I didn't have to go to every plant, 343 of them in 43 countries, and let them know, "This was serious and there's no financial limitation that should keep us from dealing with workplace hazards for the people we supposedly cared about."

And it was the beginning, it was not the end, it was the beginning of a culture developing to a point where a few years later - I'll tell you another war story - that a huge plant in Davenport, Iowa, that manufactured wings and landing gear for Boeing aircraft principally in those days. McDonnell Douglas, some companies, Northrop Grumman, had gone out of business.

Anyway, it was a huge plant, 4,000 or 5,000 people on the Mississippi River. We had a Wall Street Journal reporter who was writing a story about Alcoa. He went out to the plant on his own, rented a car at the Quad Cities Airport, and drove over to the Davenport mill.

When he got there, it was pouring down rain and so he started to get out of his car. He didn't have an umbrella, so he jumped out of the car and started running out.

A voice shouted to him, "Stop," like a bullet.

This person came running over in overalls with a big umbrella and said, "I know who you are, mister, but we really care about safety here. When you jump out of that car and get on this wet tarmac, you're likely to slip and hurt yourself. I'm going to take you over to the building where you're going, over to the administration building."

The reporter was blown away that someone unknown to an hourly worker in the Davenport plant, owns the idea of safety so strongly for anyone in their environment. That he knew that it was his duty and responsibility to protect that person who happened to be a Wall Street Journal reporter.

Incident Rates as a Leading Indicator

I tell you what, it was a major breakthrough because when I went to my first New York meeting with the New York Society of Securities Analysts after I'd been there six weeks or so, there were 250 people in a big tiered room, like a Harvard seminar room.

I was there to talk about Alcoa. I got up and said, "I want to talk to you about safety at Alcoa," and people were looking at each other, like, "He's in the wrong meeting." Or, "He had too much to drink last night or something."

I said, "Here's what I want to say to you." I said, "In Alcoa, we are going to achieve an injury-free workplace and if you want to know whether Alcoa is going to be good at anything else we do, you should pay attention to our workplace incident rates because they will be a leading indicator about whether we know what we're doing or not.

"Whether we're leading and managing the resources that are in our domain, or whether we're just riding the log down the river like most other organizations."

This created enormous buzz. They couldn't believe the CEO of Alcoa wasn't going to talk to them about financial things. Eventually, I did talk to them a little bit about financial things but related to what you all do and where you all come from. I have to tell you another thing I believe that has served me well.

> ### *In a great organization, finance is a consequence of great non-financial activity. It is not properly an independent objective.*

If you're not privileged to work in a place where people aren't running a place with financial measurements, it is a legitimate possibility to actually work on making everything perfect, which will produce better financial results than any amount of financial engineering you can conjure up in any business in the world.

I know about payment system defects and the difference between billings and reimbursements and all that stuff, and I suffer with you about what an idiotic system we live in.

But let me ask you this. If you can reduce workplace injuries, don't you think it'll make you a better place? I did.

One of the things I did when I got there and started this was calling my financial staff and say to them, "Look, this is going to work. It's going to take a while, but we are going to get better and better at not hurting people in our enterprise. Our lost work days are going to go down. Our workers' comp is going to go down.

"If any of you ever calculate how much money we saved because people don't get hurt anymore, you're fired. Because that will be the day you destroy my moral authority."

This is about caring about people in a way that is demonstrable and has nothing to do with money.

It has everything to do with creating an organization where all the human energy is aligned so that some of the things you saw today about organizations that are run by politics...

Aligning Everybody to Aspirational Goals

In my scheme of things, there's not a lot of room for what we classically call politics, or internal backbiting, or internal competition, because it's a waste of human energy that could be spent to produce the value that's there for the taking if we can align all the human beings in our organizations around aspirational goals we all share.

Who doesn't want to work in a healthcare enterprise where people never get a hospital-acquired infection?

Do we know how to get there immediately? No. But we've demonstrated in some places that I've worked with that with diligent effort and engagement of the people.

This is not about telling people how to do it, but engaging people and understanding processes of continuous learning and continuous improvement.

You can actually create a situation where central line-associated bloodstream infections are effectively zero. I'll tell you a case like that, working with Dr. Rick Shannon at Allegheny General Hospital that's up on the hill above where my office is now, which we got started in an interesting way.

When I was at Alcoa, we created something called the Alcoa University to teach people in our own enterprise ideas of continuous learning and continuous improvement. I actually asked for the people in the training activity to rename their activity from a management training program to the leadership training program. Because I believe there's a lot of difference between management and leading.

I wanted to teach people in Alcoa how to be leaders. Not how to be managers. Because I don't like the connotation, if you're a Latin scholar, that management's about manipulation. I don't like the idea of manipulation. I really like the idea of a lead population, which creates the freedom for people to contribute and have meaning in their life.

From the Veterans Administration to the Treasury

Helen challenged me a little bit to talk, not just about Alcoa, but about the public enterprise. I spent 15 years in the government. Actually, part of my early connection to health medical care, getting recruited into a management intern program at the Veterans Administration in 1961, out of graduate school, and getting recruited into a bunch of different places.

I selected to go to the VA because they offered, on the front end of my internship, 18 months of training as a computer systems analyst programmer.

Most of you are not old enough to remember this, but in 1961, what we called a computer would be laughable to you today. An IBM 1401 computer had 4,000 positions of core memory. 4,000 positions.

Anyway, it was for me, a really accidental but great choice to go get some additional skills and systems analysis and computer programming, and to understand the principles that still apply today, even though the change and conditions are just monumental today.

It was a place to begin knowing and thinking about health and medical care. Early in that career, I had an experience that really had an influence on me when I was recruited into what was then the Bureau of Budget in the Executive Office of the President.

Part of my responsibility was to oversee the budgets of public health service hospitals. In those days, there were still 32 of them that had been created in 1789 to protect the American people from merchant mariners who brought diseases back to the country.

When I landed on them in 1967 and began investigating what they were doing, I found that they had lots of infections in VA hospitals in those days that were infections that came from incompletely sterilized needles. It's still 1967, the Veterans Administration was autoclaving hypodermic needles because, from an accountant's point of view, it was cheaper than disposables, honest to God.

It's fascinating to me to see how accounting could get confused with economics and not even exist in the same world and understand the human cost of thinking about things from an accounting perspective instead of from a systems perspective that looked at the totality of an experience someone might have if they were exposed to an infection that they never should have had.

We find a manifestation of those same kinds of things, often more sophisticated today, in what we do in health and medical care. I do want to tell you a few Treasury stories. I have to lay a base by telling you one more Alcoa story.

Closing the Books Faster at Alcoa

I really did want everybody in Alcoa to be part of this idea, we're going to be the best in the world in everything we do. I called in the comptroller, Ernie Edwards, a fantastic human being.

I said to him, "Ernie, I want to know if we perfectly closed our books in this worldwide enterprise as fast as possible given the fact that we're in 43 countries, how long would it take?"

"Right now it's taking us 11 days to report our financial results to Wall Street."

"How long would it take if we did it with no repair work, no transposition of numbers, no problems with computer systems in this enterprise that owns one of every kind of computing device anybody ever created in the world, including an abacus?"

[laughter]

We had them all. I want to know if we did it perfectly, how long would it take. He came back in about three weeks.

Ernie said, "I have an answer to your question. The answer is two and a half days."

I said, "Fantastic. That should be our goal."

Ernie said, "I didn't say we could do it. It's just the answer to your question."

[laughter]

He didn't believe we could do it in two and a half days, so I said to him, this is relevant to one of the panels I attended today.

"Ernie, here are the rules. We need to examine what it is we're dredging up from around the world in 343 locations and make sure it is really necessary either to meet an SEC requirement or a New York Stock Exchange requirement or a management information requirement because we've been dragging this stuff around for 100 years."

My guess is there's a whole bunch of baggage that represents opportunities for errors that if we could skinny it down to what we really need, that would help.

Secondly, we need to get the IT people involved, and we need to say to them (I will say it to them if you don't want to do this) we need to write the computer programs so that they are intuitive to ordinary human beings, not just to computer nerds. People need to be able to sit down at their desk, and if they're part of the finance function, it needs to be intuitively obvious what we're doing.

If you need a little bit of additional resources to get this done, it's OK with me.

> **I don't think you need more resources. I think you need to engage your people in figuring out how we can do this.**

He went away muttering. In 12 months, Alcoa learned how to close its books fully closed, fully audited by insisting that the outside auditors that they had to parallel process with us. We know that's not how you do it anyplace else. It's not how you've done it here before.

I told them, "You believe you get to sit back and be the judge after we've done all the work? To hell with that. If you want to be our outside auditor, you've got to parallel process. If we're making a mistake, you help us fix it before we push it down the line and send bad product down the line. We're not going to do that anymore. 12 months, two and a half days."

Do you want to know the first company that reports its quarterly results every quarter in the United States? Alcoa. Because they stopped doing repair work.

When we started, we had 1,300 people in the finance function. Let me tell you the numbers again. From 11 days to 2.5 days. Effectively, we saved 8 days every month for 1,300 people.

First of all, they were so proud of themselves because they got validated every quarter. We are the best in the world at what we do. Then we did something I advise all of you in health and medical care to do.

When you make that kind of a breakthrough, use those brilliantly trained analytic minds to help you figure out how to get better at everything else you do.

It's not an opportunity to bring the damn patient-staffing ratios down to some world-breaking rate. It's an opportunity to apply brainpower to produce value instead of rework and aggravation.

Reducing Injuries at the Treasury Department

All right. I'm going to take you to the Treasury. Before I went to the Treasury, I had a transition meeting with Larry Summers. You probably know who Larry Summers is — he's a really famous economist. He was awarded a prize that's highly valued by economists as the smartest economist in the world under age 40. Larry won that award. He's been winning awards all his life.

Larry and I have a meeting at the JW Marriott for breakfast on a Saturday morning as we're doing the transition. Incidentally, his staff was just Sheryl Sandberg. Does anybody know who Sheryl Sandberg is? Read about her. She's a famous person who's done a great job at Facebook.

Anyway, I said to Larry, "Larry, what's the lost workday rate at the Treasury?" He said, "I don't know what you mean." Here's a person who's the head of an organization of 125,000 people. He doesn't know what the idea of the lost workday rate means.

You know why? That's not what those lofty positions have traditionally been about. It's about floating on top of your organization. It's not about really caring about the 125,000 people who work there. Sheryl said she will get me the information.

About three weeks later, they got me some data, which I honestly didn't believe. It showed that the US Treasury injury rate looked like the national average.

> ***The short end to that story is in 23 months, we reduced the injury rate of the US Treasury by 50 percent.***

You may not think IRS agents have much occupational risk, but when I say to people that health medical care is the most dangerous occupation, people stare at me with a quizzical look like, "What could be dangerous about working in a pharmacy or in the kitchen in a hospital?" They don't really understand.

There's risk, believe me, in even sedentary work, but there's also risk in places like the US Mint. When I went there the first time, the badge of honor was that you didn't have the first joint on your little finger because it got cut off in a stamping machine making pennies.

That was a badge of honor. If you haven't been here long enough to lose your little finger then you're not a veteran yet. It's not about just back strains and picking up boxes of Xerox paper and stuff like that. This is about everywhere there are risks to people.

Closing the Books Faster in the Treasury Dept

I want to tell you that finance story about the Treasury. After I've been there a few weeks, I said to the financial people, "How long does it take us to close our books at the Treasury?" They said five months.

[laughter]

I said, "Only a historian could care."

[laughter]

It has nothing to do with operational information. Why the hell are you doing it at all if it takes five months?

I said, "I know in organizations that are more complicated than yours that close the books in two and a half days. The Treasury should close its books in two and a half days, full stop."

They said, "You know, you've been out of the government for a long time."

[laughter]

They continued, "You don't know. We have laws, rules, regulations, stuff like that, that you didn't have to contend with at Alcoa. You could just dictate it."

I said, "OK, you tell me which laws, rules, and regulations are in the way of our closing our books in two and a half days. I'll get them changed." You know what? There weren't any rules, laws, or regulations.

[laughter]

Really, there were none. I got Ernie Edwards, God bless him, to come down and do a little pro bono work. Not to tell them how to do it but to teach them about the rhythm of what you all would call Lean or Six Sigma or whatever flavor you like.

> **In 12 months, the US Treasury learned how to close its books in two and a half days.**

Theoretical Limits

I've got to teach you one more concept. If you've got the patience for one more concept, I want to tell you about the idea of a theoretical limit. Here's the idea of the theoretical limit:

> **If God doesn't keep you from doing it, you can do it.**

[laughter]

I'm deadly serious.

[applause]

If you want to know how much room you have for improvement, compare everything you do to what perfect looks like, and it's like draining the swamp. How did I do what I did at Alcoa? I went out to plants and I did things like this.

I went to Cleveland where we had a 50,000-ton forging press where we stamped out landing gear for Boeing aircraft. I said to the people, just being observant and curious, "I'm really interested about how much time we cook this metal."

I'll teach you a little bit about making reliable aluminum. In order to get the properties of density and material cohesion at the molecular level that you need to produce material that's flexible, not brittle, that will stand a multi-ton aircraft coming down on the landing gear, you have to do what's called heat-treating it.

What you do is after you've rolled it out, forged it, put it into a furnace, and you cook it to a temperature for a defined period of time, it creates this bonding that you need for the right structure.

I innocently said, "I'd like to see the curves that demonstrate how the properties develop with time and temperature, so I can better understand this."

The old timer who's been around said, "Oh, you know, we learned it from the people who were here before us. We know we're doing it the right amount. We're cooking this stuff, let me say, 13 hours."

I said, "You know what, humor me a little bit. I'd like for the people in the research center to show me the curves that show that 13 hours at 1740 degrees is the right answer." They got me the curves and it turns out eight hours was the right answer.

We got back five hours' worth of time because we were overcooking material because we weren't really paying attention to the fundamentals of our process. It is latent in everything.

If you understand the idea of the theoretical limit, it causes you to be endlessly curious about, why is that? Why is it we do that the way we do? Is there a better way that would consume less resources and produce better properties, better patient outcomes?

I'd give you a bottom line. In 13 years, I don't take credit for this, I happened to be on the bridge of the ship when this happened.

We improved the market value of Alcoa, 800 percent in 13 years, by paying attention to the non-financial measures of everything we did. The non-financial measures. The finances took care of themselves.

In my exit interview with my outside auditor, he said to me, "I don't know if you're aware of it, but during the time you've been here, you've created 300 Alcoa employee millionaires." It was an artifact of a quest for excellence.

In Conclusion

Believe me — it is possible, working with empowered people who are doing the work, to achieve what we all want in a perfectly safe health and medical care enterprise. I don't have more time to convince you. I believe I could, but I think I will invite myself back next year so I can ask you again if you have a real-time safety data system for workplace safety because I will believe then that you are serious. Back at Alcoa, the financial success is going to come from process excellence, how does that change the way you manage and lead on a day-to-day basis?

Questions for Reflection and Discussion

1. What evidence is there at your organization that the workforce is indeed its most valuable asset? What steps can be taken to strengthen this commitment?

2. Why did Paul talk to this healthcare audience about closing the books more quickly at Alcoa and the Treasury? What would some benefits be from a closing-the-books type of focus or goal in your organization? What would your first such focus or goal be?

3. In your mind, is theoretical limit thinking energizing or demoralizing? Why? What is standing in your way of theoretical limit thinking in your organization?

4. In his story about "overcooking" metal at the Alcoa plant, Paul said that "endless curiosity" is part of theoretical limit thinking. What are the elements your organization needs to build or bolster to embed endless curiosity throughout? What are three tangible benefits your organization would realize if theoretical limit thinking were the way business is done?

IHI National Forum on Quality Improvement in Health Care (2003)

For this speech at the Institute for Healthcare Improvement (IHI) event, Paul was introduced by Dr. Gary Kaplan, Chairman and CEO of Virginia Mason Medical Center, based in Seattle. Dr. Kaplan has personally led the patient safety improvement work and the "Virginia Mason Production System" efforts for almost 20 years.

Gary, thank you very much for the introduction. I have to tell you all because you can't sense it from where you are, I've got this blazing light — I can't see your eyes, and I really don't like that. It's difficult to talk to people without being able to see what their eyes are taking in, and slow down or speed up your pace so that you're connecting with people.

For me, it's a great privilege to have an opportunity to engage you all today. It's a large audience. But I hope I can speak informally enough that I engage you individually. I must tell you I love the theme of this conference. The theme of courage. It seems, to me, just right.

What's the North Star?

And for me, it's difficult not to start at the beginning. So, let me start at what is the beginning for me when I think about health and medical care. In fact, when I think more broadly about our society, it's a habit of mind to begin with "what's the North Star?"

Or maybe said in a different way, "What's the ideal condition that one could imagine?" And I would suggest to you it does take some courage to not get lost in the weeds but to begin by having the courage to imagine what our society would be like if it were in fact ideal.

So, when I say to myself, what's the ideal we should be striving for as a society? In health and medical care, I would say close to the top of the list is that there should be meaning to the notion of being an American when it comes to health and medical care.

And, for me, that meaning at the top would be that every American has access to the health and medical care that they need, without regard to income or wealth.

But there's a question then, how do we achieve that? And I believe there's an answer to that question. In fact, in 1975 President Ford included, in his legislative program for the Congress, a proposal to create a catastrophic health insurance for Americans, where catastrophic was defined not the traditional way, but in reference to individuals' combination of income and wealth status. Recognizing that catastrophic for someone who has nothing begins with the first dollar. Catastrophic for someone who has a lot of financial means begins much later.

I continue to believe that was the correct idea. And that, in an ideal society, access will be available to all. And we will recognize a fundamental principle which we seem to forget with regularity now. And that is, that government doesn't have any money it doesn't first take away from us.

So, when you follow the logic trail, what that means is that individuals of means have a responsibility to provide for and have the financial means to pay for their own health and medical care and, in a just society, to pay a proportional share for those who don't have the means to provide their own access. Frankly, I think we would be advantaged if we could keep that simple frame in mind as we think about what we should be doing as we go forward.

A National Medical Record for Each of Us

I do think there are some things that we need to do at the national level. And let me start with one that I think is maybe a step beyond what Don [Berwick, MD, CEO of IHI] said to us yesterday about individuals having their own medical records and x-rays.

I believe this — we need a national standard for capturing health and medical care information about every individual American and we should begin collecting it when people are in the fetus stage. And the information should reside in cyberspace. And it should include digital captures of everything about us having to do with health and medical care, including x-rays and MRIs and CT scans and all the rest.

And you'll note I didn't say federal, I said national because I do think we need a standard that's not driven by some notion of government, but a standard that's driven by a notion of if we captured all the information in a usable way, what would that standard look like?

And then imagine, if you will, going to a provider outside of your home area and giving that provider your four-digit code that allowed that provider to look at everything that's ever been recorded or known about you, including allergies and the contraindications of multiple drugs and, whatever had affected you and been recorded about you, lab tests and all the rest.

This technological capability we already have.

And I, in fact, talked to [Secretary of Health and Human Services] Tommy Thompson about putting this kind of a national standard out there for all of us.

First of all, maybe in the first six months or so to shoot at, so that we refine it to a level that we can have an agreement that yes this is the way we're going to do it. What I see in the absence of this is, in our own case and I think that many of yours, people working on the edges of this issue in the absence of a national standard for gathering information, collecting information, and making it available.

So, for example, at the University of Pittsburgh Medical Center system, we've embarked on and are nearing the end of a $500 million investment in a proprietary standard. You know, it's not worthy, I think, of what we could do and what could happen if we had this kind of an information set available.

I would quickly add I do think we need, at the same time, that we create this national standard of how to collect information, a much-strengthened privacy law that basically does this — that says all of that information that's collected about us, we own. The providers don't own it, we own it.

So, it gets to the issue that Don was talking to us about yesterday, of him having become a felon in order to get all of his x-rays. You know, and with this notion of data capture, no one's a felon, and every American citizen owns as personal property their own information about their health and medical status, and they can make it available to providers to the degree, and with the sweep, that they choose. This is an important thing we need to do as a precondition for moving down to the operating level.

A National Error Reporting System

There are a couple of other things that we need. We need what, for me, seems a simple concept, a prejudice toward telling the truth about things gone wrong. And I would do this in this way.

I would have Congress, and maybe state legislators, pass a law that says if something goes wrong in the provision of care, it ought to be appropriately identified and recorded and communicated in the appropriate way within 24 hours. And if it's done within 24 hours, we the society basically will warrant to any individual who's harmed by an intervention gone wrong, we will warrant to those individuals, the actual economic costs that they suffer.

And in the event that something goes wrong, and it's identified but not reported within 24 hours, that the damages can be trebled or quadrupled so that we have an incentive for telling the truth and telling it fast.

Now, why do I make this case?

Because I don't believe it's possible to have rapid continuous constructive learning unless one identifies everything gone wrong as quickly as possible and acts on it.

And so, I think it's much in our interest if we could help the Congress to see the importance of giving all of us an incentive to tell the truth and tell it fast.

There's one other thing we need from the national level. We need an outcry from all of us, that says the reimbursement system that we live with now is the height of cynicism and we don't choose to live with it anymore.

You know the experience I've had in other walks of life; I don't know of another case where people accept as a norm reimbursements at a 40% rate related to the initial billings, and they consider that a normal state of affairs. You know, why do I tackle that issue?

Because I believe it's very difficult for organizations to achieve true greatness if their everyday work is surrounded by cynicism.

And for me, the reimbursement system is the height of cynicism. I think it didn't start with that motivation, but I think it's unfortunate that that's where we are today.

Let me move then from things we need from the national level or from the federal level to what it is I believe we need to do to create this access notion that I suggested. I believe, I think many of you have done work that undergirds this notion, that with a $1.4 trillion that we're now spending every year on health and medical care that we're only getting about 50% of the value that's associated with the inputs.

The Potential for Greatness and the Limits of Our Potential

Let me say it more sharply to you. I believe, maybe you don't, that if we operated at the limit of our potential in terms of doing everything right every time in every encounter between providers and patients, that we could reduce the cost of medical care by 50% and simultaneously see an enormous improvement in the health care status of individuals. It's not easy to do or we already would have done it. But I do believe it is possible to move in that direction and to move there quickly.

Now you might wonder "how do we do it?" I have to tell you, I believe that it's hard to find examples of institutions or organizations achieving goals that they haven't aspired to.

And so, I'm one who believes you start with a notion of setting goals at the theoretical limit of what's possible.

And so, to take individual examples, I believe it's possible to perform in such a way that there are zero medication errors, and the zero nosocomial infections, and zero readmissions of CABG patients, and whatever else you'd like to imagine could be, and ought to be, zero.

And I have to tell you, it is really a privilege to address this audience because all of you in one way or another are leaders and yesterday, we talked a little bit about "what are you going to do on Monday morning?"

I would hope on Monday morning, wherever you fit in this puzzle, you would think about what's the description of a theoretical limit that you as a leader can and should put in place. Because I think without that beginning it's awfully hard to set your course and keep it straight every day.

Gary [Kaplan] mentioned safety at Alcoa. And one of the things that I've hammered away at as I've been involved directly in health and medical care is to try to get people in this business, the health and medical care business, to understand both the notion of the theoretical limit and why it is valuable to think about the safety of people who are providers.

Let me see if I can connect the logic for you. Again, this is for you who are leaders.

I think organizations only have the potential for greatness if the people in the organizations can say yes without any reservation every day to three propositions.

1. The first proposition is I'm treated with dignity and respect every day by everyone I encounter. They would be able to say "yes" to that. And let me say that means without regard to educational attainment, or rank, or ethnicity, or any other identifier that we all have — that you can say every day without any reservation I'm treated with dignity and respect by everyone I encounter.

2. Secondly, that everyone in the organization can say every day without any reservation — I'm given the education, and training, and encouragement, and tools that I need in order to make a contribution — and this is the important part — that gives meaning to my life. Not that makes the organization more profitable or something, that I'm able to make the contribution that gives meaning to my life.

3. And the third proposition is people need to be able to say "yes" to is that someone noticed that I did it.

In any organization I know of that has real greatness or the potential for greatness, the people in it can say yes to those three propositions every day.

And then there is a potential for doing great things together. Without that, it's very difficult. And then let me connect that to what I said to you about the theoretical limits and let me use medication errors as an example for connection.

Theoretical Limits

At least in my experience, as I wander around and look at the medication error problem, I think that we're still limited by prescribers, by doctors, who think it's not their duty to write in a legible way or to eliminate abbreviations.

What I would say to you about that is — the highest form of disrespect one person can pay to another is to basically say I'm better than you — maybe not articulated this way, but by action — to say to the recipient of a scribble, "It's your problem if you can't read it."

Now why I tell you all of that is because there are some things that we need to do together. Because as I pushed on this issue, some hospital administrators have said to me, "I know we shouldn't let this happen in our organization" — that where we have habitual cases, where the order writer refuses to make it bulletproof, that we're not going to have any mistakes because of misinterpretation.

If I really put down the hammer, sometimes the people who are habitual abusers will say, "Fine, if that's the way it's going to be, I'll take my patients someplace else."

You know if we, for example in Southwestern Pennsylvania or you wherever you are as a community, had the will to say in our community, maybe 40 or 50 or 100 hospitals, we're going to band together and we're all going to put down the law that is not okay to create the danger that's resident in us, in a scribbled order, the people who would abuse each other and show no respect for the recipient of their orders wouldn't have any place to go.

That takes some working together. And I must tell you I really do believe there is a lot that we should and want to do to work together on what I call a pre-competitive collaboration. Now, let me see if I can illustrate for you what I mean by that.

Gary [Kaplan] told you that at Alcoa we became one of the safest companies in the world. That's not quite right.

We became THE safest company in the world.

How did we do it? Let me go back to what I said to you at the beginning about information systems.

The Role of Leaders

We created what I call the "real time safety information system." And we had a requirement in our organization — 36 countries and 350 locations — that in the event anyone had an injury including a first aid injury, it would be identified and recorded within 24 hours.

The people that were involved would work together as a team to identify the root cause of the problem, and it would be put into cyberspace for 140,000 people to learn from within 24 hours — so that we didn't have to learn the same lesson over and over and over again, one institution at a time, one location at a time. We had the capacity to take one incident and turn it into learning for 140,000 people.

And one of the things that I must tell you I'm most proud of at Alcoa is that when I left the lost workday rate was 0.2, which means statistically you could work at Alcoa for 800 years without having a lost workday case.

Today the lost workday rate at Alcoa is 0.12, which means they got better after I left.

> ***And I would suggest to you a real mark of leadership is whether the organization you left behind is better after you've left then when you left.***

In a nutshell, what that's all about is systemic change. It's not about dictated change or change as a consequence of an autocrat. It's about the enablement of systemic change, which I believe is the real role of leaders.

There are a couple of other things I believe about leadership.

> ***One is that true leaders believe that they're responsible for everything, especially for things gone wrong.***

They'll get the credit for things gone right maybe. But I think leaders should really have a sense of burden so that for example, if you're a hospital administrator and something goes wrong in your institution, it's not because someone else didn't do the right thing, it's because you didn't lead properly.

Because, at least in most organizations, if you're the leader, you have the responsibility to identify the people and give them training education they need, give them the tools that they need. And if something goes wrong, it's not their fault it's your fault — there's something wrong in how you exercise your leadership.

So I think leaders need to have this important notion, that they're the standup people who accept, along with the right to make decisions, the responsibility to be at the end of the line for everything that happens in the institution and therefore, not only to set goals at the theoretical limit but to create the conditions and the processes so that everyone in the organization can let their energy flow toward achieving the theoretical limits.

> *One of the things that's really important*
> *for leaders to do is to take away excuses.*

And as we have worked on these issues of quality, in the broadest sense, in Pittsburgh, I found the same set of excuses that I found at Alcoa when I started talking about how our organization could achieve this unique condition of no one ever being hurt. And the excuses go like this — these are without regard to the industry or institution — they're always the same.

The first set of excuses is "it's not possible." You know, for example, people will say, "What we want to do is eliminate unnecessary infections." You know, I don't like the modifier. "Unnecessary," for me, may, in fact, be a cause that we haven't yet figured out how to eliminate.

But once you permit your mind to believe that some things are unavoidable, you'll never work on the problem. So, we need to be clear about not having modifiers. And for example, again in the area of safety, language is important.

One of the things that I worked hard on at Alcoa was to get the language right. If you think about the implications of the word "accident," it has with it the notion that it's nobody's fault. But if you change the characterization of things gone wrong to "incident," then we can work on it.

And I would warrant this to you — God didn't decide we should hurt ourselves. And therefore, theoretical limits need to be set within the boundaries of what God will permit us to do and to imagine, and not to forgive ourselves for not having the answers. That's how you achieve what I believe is true greatness in an organization.

Leaders Need to Take Away the Excuses

Once you've done that, again you need to work on the excuses. People will say, "We can't afford it, it's not in the budget." And again, one of the things for leaders to do is take away excuses.

How do you do that? By saying you know that I'm so confident that we can accomplish this ideal state that when we identify a root cause that costs us some money to eliminate hazards for workers, we're going to fix it immediately. We're not going to hide behind "it's not in the budget." It's more important than anything and everything else and therefore we're going to fix it right now.

That might seem a little scary to you. Believe me, it works. It really does work to take away the excuses.

And then you find out it doesn't cost a lot of money to do things right. It takes systems, organization, and the will of the people.

I labor you hard on the subject of safety for this reason. Because I want to get you to a point of hopefully agreement that providers' safety is something we should work at.

Let me tell you the facts about the health and medical care industry in the United States. According to the most recent data, which is at the end of last year, the lost workday rate in health and medical care delivery people in the United States is 3.3. That's 27 times higher than Alcoa where the metal flows at 2000 degrees and there's clanking, moving overhead machinery.

> ***I would say to you, there's no excuse for healthcare providers to have an injury rate that is 27 times higher than it's already been demonstrated it's possible to be.***

And so, when I go when I look at the dashboards people are creating about measures of effectiveness, which is an advancing state and what's going on in medical care in the United States. You know, it's been very hard for me to find any dashboard that includes provider safety. And I'm really puzzled by that.

Go Find Your Own Facts

And one of the things I hope my conversation with you this morning will cause you to do is to find out what your own facts are. You know, I'm just startled to find as I go and talk to hospital administrators and people who have thousands of people working for them, they haven't got a clue about what's happening with their own staff.

And again, I would say to you, if you can't find that people are connected together by this notion of "first of all we will make sure that we're okay," then it's unlikely that they're going to achieve true organizational greatness because they haven't yet tended to the thing that should draw us all together in common cause.

Now the reason I press on this, as well, is because there's no way to get to zero without using what we call the quality tools of data gathering, data analysis, root cause analysis, and a common agreement on goal to get there.

It's the same reason that as we started with Pittsburgh Regional Health Initiative, thinking long and hard about what our goals should be, we said let's do medication errors and nosocomial infections.

Both are measurable. Particularly medication errors, I think, are clearly measurable. And in order to get to zero, one needs the same set of systems ideas and analytic tools to get to zero. And so, it's not so much that medication errors or nosocomial infections are the beginning and end of what we should aspire to, but...

... getting to zero in either one of those measures will cause our organizations to employ the tools that are necessary for greatness in everything.

And I would say to you, that should be our real goal together. Not that we have isolated examples of superior performance on a project basis, but that what we are truly dedicated to is systemic change and organizations that bristle with continuous learning and continuous improvement. And I believe if we can get on that path, we can accomplish a lot in a hurry.

Now, the fact suggests to me, frankly, that we have a long way to go, but we could make enormous progress in a hurry if we bend our will to it. Lucian Leape [MD] has done some analysis that says there are 300 million medication errors in the United States every year, broadly defined. And I think the scope of his definition includes way beyond a medication error that hurt a patient or endangered a patient.

They include all of the times when a pharmacist has to call to find out what was really intended and every other wasted activity that goes along with an imperfect system. And that suggests, for example, in our part of the country in Pittsburgh that we should be reporting three million errors a year. And right now, we're reporting about 15,000.

I think this is the gulf between where we are and where we ought to be in first, identifying a thing gone wrong or things gone potentially wrong, so that we can work together on root causes and eliminate the possibility of things going wrong. And so, it would be remarkable if a year from now, across this country we could be reporting all the medication errors or all the nosocomial infections, because it would be a beginning signal that we're serious about what we say we want to do.

We need the facts that confirm our words, and to demonstrate that we have a serious purpose. And there are places where this has happened.

I was in one of our hospitals in the last few weeks. I like being on the ground, and the people were showing me the last two and a half years of data for patient falls. And the first two years was what most of you probably have. It was a very low rate, and it was pretty stable. In the last six months, the rate has skyrocketed. And not because they have more patient falls but because they've decided to report and record all falls, including those where the patient isn't hurt.

And as a consequence of that one little twist of how to think about the problem, they've been able to do an analysis with this big increase in reported incidents of "why are these things happening?"

And what they found is most of these incidents are happening during a shift change, where the incomings and the outgoings are conferring with each other, and patients are left to their own devices to get into and out of bed if they need to. And so, they recognize that they need to staff to the patient need — that is to say be available when patients need them, not when it's convenient in the context of the way we've structured our process so that there's a gap and availability during shift changes.

These are the kind of things on the ground that can happen if we begin to report everything. And again, to link back to the reason for this notion of an incentive system that rewards telling the truth fast.

Part of the reason I think we're not getting the kind of full-scale reporting we ought to is because of fear that if we tell the truth, we're going to get in trouble. And I must say to you, tomorrow is a year since I've left the Treasury. And yeah, I've been saying as

I've met with audiences over the last year, I am an example of a biblical injunction which says "the truth shall set you free." So that there is some risk in telling the truth. But let me say to you at least as one witness, it's worth it.

Not only is it worth it, I think, in telling the truth, getting every incident out there where we can learn from it, is an essential ingredient of making quick progress.

Because again in my experience, you know when we started a safety quest at Alcoa, in the first 18 or 24 months we reduced our rate 50% simply because we began paying attention and learning from our experience. And every year after that was an improvement of 30% to 50% from where we began the previous year.

I have the absolute confidence that the same thing can happen in health and medical care, in the most complex processes, and therefore this sense of urgency about reporting everything and doing it fast.

Now, I want to do a little commercial for one of the things I was privileged to see yesterday. The CEO, chairman, and president of Virginia Mason made a presentation to the CEO forum that was really striking to this degree.

They talked about their determination to use all of the tools and ideas of the Toyota Production System to guide their process of achieving excellence at Virginia Mason.

I was really struck because it was a commitment without an exit door, which I believe is essential. You know if we're going to make

93

really good rapid progress, we can't do what we said we want to do on a pilot, let's see how it works, basis. This needs to be "the" way we're going to proceed — not "a" way we're going to proceed and hope it works right.

Maybe one more thought to share with you which I said to the Leadership Obligation Group in Pittsburgh Regional Health Initiative earlier this week — I believe those of us who are working on these issues of quality and excellence in health and medical care, need to soon have — not just the individual illustrations that Don [Berwick] gave us yesterday, which many of us know from our own experience of areas of excellence in different institutions around the country — we need to have convincing communicable evidence on an institution-wide basis that these ideas and tools produce the values that some of us think are potentially there so that others will have the courage to follow.

And we need it soon.

I frankly don't believe that we should accept the notion that this is a task for the generations. Because if we make it a task for the generations, we're never going to get it done. It needs to be "what we're going to do on Monday morning?" And for me, that's a real question for all of us. As a consequence of spending these days together, I hope you will ask yourself as you go away,

> ***"What am I personally going to do different on Monday morning that will hasten our progress down this path?"***

The Courage to Lead

And then one last word. Take with you the courage to lead. It is the most important thing, that we not wait for someone else to lead. You individually need to be the leaders who achieve the vision that Don [Berwick] shared with us yesterday of being a great society.

Maybe to link back, if you don't mind, 40 years. I went to Washington in 1961 and it seems a little corny now to remember why I went. But I suppose I was enough of an idealist in 1961 when John Kennedy said, "If you want to make a difference, come here." I believe that.

And I also believed that what we can achieve is what we can imagine, and not what we've inherited, and not what we're limited to by conventions and practices, and the traditional practices. And so, as you have the courage to lead, I hope you will link back maybe 40 years to a simpler time and imagine what an ideal world looks like, and do your part to get us there. Thank you very much.

Questions for Reflection and Discussion

1. What would be the ideal condition in your organization? What steps can you take to ensure you have a clear understanding of your current condition, to assess against the ideal condition? What would a plan to close gaps look like?

2. What do you need to do to leave your organization better than when you arrived? Why is that important to you? How can you set your organization up to continue improving after your departure?

3. What excuses have you encountered (or given), or do you think would be given, when theoretical limit ideas are put forward? What can your organization do to eliminate such excuses?

4. What can you personally do Monday morning to hasten progress of the path your organization is on? How will you begin?

Invited Testimony — U.S. Senate Committee on Finance (2006)

Introduction by Ken Segel, co-founding principal and managing director of Value Capture:

In March of 2006, when Paul O'Neill received an invitation from Senate Finance Committee Chairman Charles Grassley to testify before his committee on the subject of healthcare, he jumped at the chance.

The hearing was titled "Taking a Checkup on the Nation's Health Care Tax Policy: A Prognosis," and through it Senator Grassley and Senator Max Baucus, the minority chair, were hoping to spark a rethink of health care finance policy given the escalating dismal impacts escalating costs were having on Americans' economic well being, competitiveness, and health.

They called only three witnesses: O'Neill, a former US Treasury Secretary, CEO of Alcoa and leader in the health care safety movement first, followed by a think tank leader from the Urban Institute, and the CEO of John Deere & Co.

Grassley knew why he wanted O'Neill on the witness list. In his introduction, the Senator not only cited O'Neill's "extensive career in government and the private sector [that] has required him to consider Americans' health care policy from multiple perspectives" and also noted that O'Neill "was a person in this town who was always willing to deliver bad, as well as good news... One thing we need in this town is someone who says it like it is, because this is kind of a good news town, and when you hear only good news, that is why problems do not get solved in this town."

As he began his testimony, O'Neill noted that Grassley should have just referred to him as a "professional iconoclast" and then tried to live up to the label not only of "telling it like it is" but "telling it like it could be" in all the best ways.

The statement offered O'Neill a chance to pull together all of his experience and achievements to explain how American health care policy and delivery could be reframed and rethought, based on a return to "first principles." He also explained how the same thinking would have to also extend to fundamental tax reform and the social policy system, to together enable great progress for the standing of the American people.

After his statement, O'Neill was immediately invited back to Washington for further meetings with the Senators and their staffs.

O'Neill's stirring framing, his powerful examples and evidence provided to support his positions, makes for a powerful, thought-provoking prescription and great reading to this day.

Mr. Chairman and Members of the Committee:

It is an honor to be asked to testify before this distinguished body on an issue of such vital interest to the future of our Republic. American health care policy is in desperate need of reframing and rethinking based on a return to first principles. This committee sits at the intersection of policy issues that must be acted on together in order to produce a coherent and workable framework for a better future for Americans and America.

Fundamental tax reform, financial security for retirees and access to medical care for all Americans are not separate subjects. In the absence of coordinated policy and legislative action by this Committee, there is no hope.

Three Primary Imperatives

There are three primary imperatives.

First, stop tinkering at the margins of a variety of ill-defined problems with tax policy. Refocus finance policy simply and powerfully on the biological human need at the core of all of this: ensuring that every American has access to health care services, equitably and efficiently.

To do so, I would pass a law mandating every American to purchase a base level of health care coverage. Those that have a certain level of income and wealth must not only carry coverage, but through a simplified, fundamentally reformed tax system, provide financial support to help those who don't have the means to fully finance their own coverage. This step would pierce several myths that serve to obscure our path forward in healthcare finance. These include the notion that the government creates social benefits from some magic pot of money that it doesn't first take from the people.

A second paralyzing myth is that employers provide health care benefits, rather than the reality that they take dollars that would otherwise be available for compensation and act as a rather inefficient and increasingly spotty pass-through for insurance benefits. If we enacted my approach, the resources to pay for health care stay attached to the people who generate them, insurance assumes its proper role as a spreader of the financial risk associated with uneven distribution of illness and incidents, and society can succeed in ensuring equal access to health care services for every American, which is the entire point.

(To make this work, the insurance market must again be required to perform its social purpose — spreading the financial risk that is associated with the uneven distribution of illness and injuries, rather than remain the risk-avoidance industry that policymakers have allowed it to become.)

My second set of recommendations flow from the truth that achieving full access to health care for everyone in society is in part a function of how much health care costs. Unless we get more value from each dollar we invest, we are unlikely to achieve access for every American.

> *On this front, the evidence is increasingly clear that if health care providers performed at the theoretical limit of organizational performance, we could reduce the costs of care by 30%–50%, while substantially improving outcomes.*

Yet, the federal government has only tip-toed toward the ideas and approaches to capture value on this scale that have been demonstrated in every field of human endeavor. I am proud to say that we had success of this scale during my time as CEO of Alcoa, and that I have been part of early demonstrations that this is possible in health care.

To achieve those 30%–50% gains across the country, this body should ensure that health care performance goals are set that are worthy of this nation, and that the conditions of transparency and accountability necessary for rapid learning and improvement are fully in place for the quality of care, for the cost of care, and for learning from "things gone wrong" (safety).

I'll provide details on these conditions later in my testimony. But let me highlight one recommendation to jump-start the nation. I would immediately fund a study of five outstanding American hospitals that systematically details how all of their operations are performing when measured against perfection, and indicates the process problems that create the gaps between the current performance of any particular process and the ideal.

Since 1999, when the Institute of Medicine pierced our national complacency regarding the safety and performance problems that afflict our hospitals, the industry and policymakers alike have seemed paralyzed about what to do to close the gap. The type of "Total Value Opportunity Study"[5] I describe is a tool used often in private enterprise to map how to actually gain safety, quality and cost improvements of the scale we need, and I believe it could provide the missing "connective tissue" for health care.

---

[5] See the Appendix after these remarks

My third imperative is to embrace the connections between solving this problem and solving the other social dilemmas that rest squarely in the lap of this Committee.

For example, I have advocated a "return to first principles" approach to solving the Social Security shortfall, in the Los Angeles Times, and in numerous speeches and interviews.

Here is the basic premise. If we invested $23,000 on the day each American child was born and allowed the magic of compounding to do its work, when that child turned 65 years old they would have an annuity in excess of $1,000,000 to support their life needs. This assumes a very conservative 6% annual rate of return. The level of income such an annuity would throw off (in excess of $80,000 per year) would give real meaning to the idea of financial security for every American retiree by providing completely for all of their needs, including health care, food, clothing, shelter and transportation.

In short, if this body commits to stop trafficking in fictions with the American people, and commits to anchor finance policies to the most economically efficient ways to produce value, you have a chance to transform the vast and certain human pain associated with our present social dilemmas into American success stories that will be recognized for generations.

How to Capture the Lost Value

Before elaborating on the conditions necessary to capture the 30%–50% value that is presently being lost in health care activities, let me provide some background on my standing to address the topic.

Many of you know that my involvement and interest in health and medical care spans more than four decades. Early in my career, at the Veterans Administration, I created some of the first systems analysis models to help optimize the health care that our veterans received. At the President's Office of the Budget, I helped create an analytic system for considering what investments could give the federal government the most return for its dollar in actually improving health care outcomes. I was also responsible, with some of you and your predecessors, for implementing a few of the major health care programs that have done so much good for the American people, but have also had such significant unforeseen consequences.

After leaving the Ford Administration, I set out to test in the private sector the ideas that I believed could lead to the creation of great value across any dimension of human activity — great social value, great human value, and great economic value.

In my second assignment, as CEO of Alcoa, I got the chance to put my ideas fully into practice. I committed myself and the company to the notion that we could become the best at everything we did by committing ourselves to becoming the first injury-free workplace in the world.

Much like this Committee may be doing at this moment, Wall Street scratched its head for years at the notion that human values, safety performance and financial success could somehow be connected.

Yet, as we progressed toward our goal of complete safety, we gained the human bonds and the deep skills at understanding and improving our processes that every one of our people applied to transform us from a threatened company in 1987 to an increase of 800% in market value by 2000, an increase that was sustained through the bursting of the economic bubble.

We did become the safest company to work for in the world, despite the presence of tremendous hazards in the workplace, and the fact that we were more than 120,000 people working in more than 30 countries, many with terrible health and safety records. Today, Alcoa's lost workday rate is more than twenty-seven times smaller than the average American healthcare institution.

What I understood — and Wall Street didn't — is that it is people that produce value in any enterprise, and that people will respond to a set of values and proven ideas and principles to produce unbelievable increases in performance.

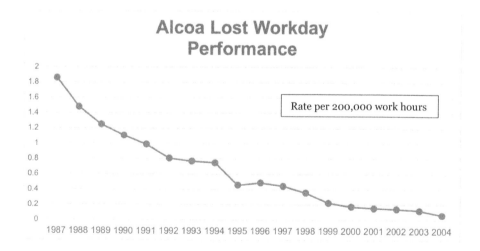

Alcoa Lost Workday Performance

Rate per 200,000 work hours

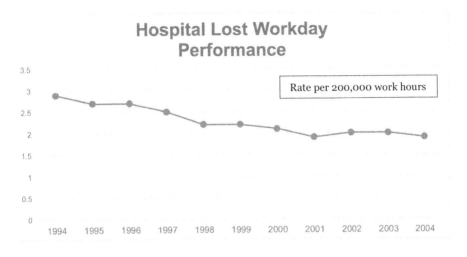

Hospital Lost Workday Performance

Rate per 200,000 work hours

As Alcoa flourished, I felt that I had proven my hypothesis regarding what ideas would create true social value across very complex enterprises, in any discipline. The sector in our society that was obviously crying out for rapid improvement was health care.

Accordingly, in 1998 I joined other leaders in Pittsburgh to create the Pittsburgh Regional Healthcare Initiative, one of the most ambitious efforts to radically improve the performance of the health care system in the United States. We set out to eliminate healthcare-acquired infections and medication errors within three years.

What we did achieve was notable — a more than 65% drop in central-line associated bloodstream infections, widespread sharing of information on medication errors, and stronger community learning systems in heart surgery, among other areas.

But while many in Pittsburgh were satisfied with this rate of improvement, including our largest hospital system and academic medical center, I was not, because they were not comprehensive or embedded as new ways to think and work in the DNA of the organizations.

I believe we need three to five health care institutions where the leaders are determined to use the ideas of systems analysis in every aspect of their enterprises to act as model sites for the rest of the nation to learn what it will really take to solve our health care crisis on a sustainable basis.

Accordingly, a year ago I and a few associates founded a small enterprise named Value Capture to partner with just a few health care CEOs around the country to help them achieve these results. We are working with Richard Salluzzo, MD, CEO of the Wellmont Health System in Eastern Tennessee, and Cliff Orme, the CEO of LifeCare Hospitals of Pittsburgh, and considering engagements with several others.

> ***In working with these determined leaders,***
> ***we have yet to observe a process that***
> ***could not be improved by a minimum of 50%.***

How the Federal Government Can Help

Having provided this background, here are more detailed recommendations for my second imperative: how the federal government can create the conditions necessary to capture 30%–50% better return on our investments in health care through the applications of systems principles to health care operations.

1. *Set national performance goals at the limit of what is theoretically possible, focusing on safety and quality, and pursue them with vigor.*

Unfortunately, the federal government rarely sets performance targets at all, let alone setting them at the theoretical limit of human attainment. The result of not insisting on the elimination of fundamental problems with the performance of the healthcare system is more of the same, or worse.

For example, there are clear reasons that the appalling healthcare-acquired infection rate — affecting approximately one in 12 people admitted to the hospital — has been steady or increasing for decades.

The only common database that comes close to a shared learning system for these infections has been the Centers for Disease Control's NNIS system, which due to lack of mandate and budget constraints has covered less than one-tenth of the nation's hospitals. Within that database, infection types constituting more than 50% of the total number of infections that occur in hospitals are not counted at all. Unsound "cost-benefit" reasoning is used to justify this exclusion. This is a sorry state of affairs.

Yet, if the federal government were to say that we are determined as a nation to eliminate healthcare-associated infections within five years, and make sure each leader in the system, from the head of Medicare to each hospital CEO, were held accountable for establishing the urgent and comprehensive learning systems necessary to make rapid progress, the glaring inadequacies of our present efforts and thought processes would be quickly surfaced and flushed out of the system.

I'd like to stress the importance of carefully structured accountability. National goals that are just slogans are useless, even dangerous.

I strongly recommend focusing national performance goals on safety and quality measures, despite the fact that driving out waste to make healthcare access affordable is an integral objective. Health care organizations to date have reacted to cost pressures by driving themselves by goals unrelated to the quality of their care. Measures derived from perverse financial incentives, such as "average length of stay," dominate the industry.

These goals are not rooted in human biology and healing, the very point of the healthcare system. Accordingly, focusing on them threatens to destroy value rather than create it, by creating incentives for behaviors unassociated or disassociated from healing.

In addition, the healthcare workforce is much less motivated by cost savings than they are by improving care for patients, and by their own safety. This reflects the truth we demonstrated at Alcoa; give people goals that they find motivating, and they will apply the skills they learn in pursuit of them to every aspect of their work lives, including the financial aspects of the enterprise.

I also strongly urge you to set our nation's goals at perfection.

Setting Goals at the Theoretical Limit

Most organizations make the mistake of establishing arbitrary benchmarks to define success. It is particularly glaring that benchmarking accepts a certain level of error or poor quality as "normal" when it comes to basic safety for patients in our health care system. If our goal would be to have "just" 4% of patients contract an infection while they're in the hospital to be cured, who among us will volunteer to be among the 4%?

First in Pittsburgh, and now with a few health systems around the country, we're aiming at the "theoretical limit" of perfection, healthcare systems with zero hospital-acquired infections, zero medication errors, and the world's best patient outcomes in clinical areas like cardiac surgery, diabetes, depression, and obstetrics.

We think those goals defuse defensiveness and blame, and keep people pushing forward. The question isn't whether we are "good" or "bad." It is, "What's the next step toward perfect?" It also drives one toward thinking, "How could we be sure this is done right every time?"

Finally, one reason most organizations don't set perfection as the goal (and so don't try to reach it), is that they believe that it costs too much to address the last few percentage points of error.

This doctrine is enshrined by economists as the "law of diminishing returns" and also afflicts notions of federal spending priorities. Unfortunately, it's untrue and dangerous.

The best organizations understand that excellence comes from getting really good at making improvements and solving problems "on the shop floor." They know that as they get toward zero defects, their progress tends to accelerate because they have built the capability and support systems for their staffs to excel.

Is progress on this scale possible in health care? Yes. Our associate Rick Shannon, MD, Chief of Medicine at one of Pittsburgh's largest academic medical centers, Allegheny General Hospital, has created a profound case study.

Under his leadership, the ICUs he controls used systems principles to reduce one type of infection rate by 95%. How long did it take? Less than 90 days. How long has it been sustained? For more than two-and-a-half years.

The approach has now spread to the hospital's other ICUs, and several other infection types. The financial impact on the hospital has been profound. To date, the efforts have saved the institution more than $2 million. We see similar gains being realized across a number of systems problems with our current partners at LifeCare and Wellmont Health System in Tennessee.

And Pittsburgh has shown that even with basic levels of cooperation and learning, infection rates will quickly fall by more than 60%.

The elimination of these problems is possible everywhere. But it won't happen everywhere until this government, led by this Committee, insists on it.

Once safety and quality goals are set, transparent reporting on progress down to the level of specific institutions is a useful accelerant. The early efforts of CMS to publicize health system performance across a few measures should be radically expanded. A few farsighted institutions are far ahead of the pack on recognizing that comprehensive disclosure of performance is helpful to the fulfillment of their mission. I would urge you to examine the safety and quality reporting of the Norton Health Care System in Kentucky at www.nortonhealthcare.com for an example.

2. *Commission a National Total Value Opportunity Study*

I specified in the introduction to my testimony that a "Total Value Opportunity" study at five of the nation's leading health care institutions could ignite actual progress toward safety and quality goals across American health care by providing a much more concrete picture of where in specific health care processes much greater value can be captured, and specifying the "real world" improvements in the processes that would capture that value.

By doing the study at acknowledged centers of excellence of various types (academic health centers, community and rural health systems), the results could not be dismissed.

Experts trained in systems analysis (six sigma, lean manufacturing, Toyota Production System, activity-based costing) would be paired with medical authorities to conduct the study, which could be accomplished within 6–9 months of work at each institution.

To give you a sense of the picture that such a study would paint, here are process diagrams showing A) a typical hospital medication process, from the time the physician writes the order to the time the medicine is actually delivered to the patient; B) a far simpler, safer and more efficient "target condition" imagined by staff at the same institution.

CURRENT CONDITION

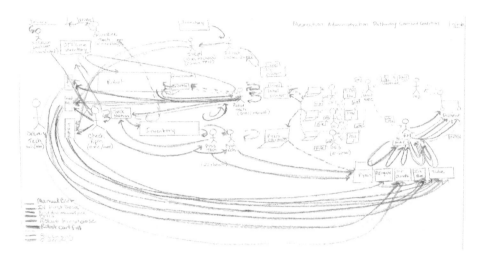

TARGET CONDITION

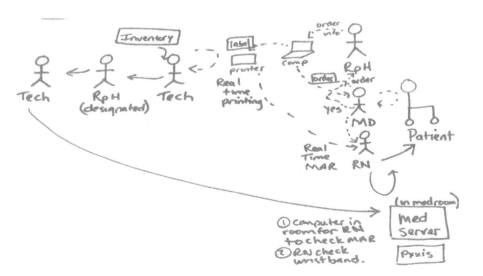

And here are two slides summarizing the clinical and financial implications of dramatic improvements in another process, infection control, produced by Dr. Shannon at Allegheny General Hospital in work that is an early prototype for the type of study I have proposed. The national study should associate each possible process improvement with resource consumption and finance implications:

The Losses Attributable to CLABs are Staggering

- Average reimbursement: $64,894
- Average Expense: $91,733
- Average Loss from Operations: -$26,839
- Total Loss from Operations: -$1,406,901
- Average Age: 56 years
- Average LOS: 28 days (5-86)
- Only three patients were discharged to home!

	Traditional Approach FY 03	PPC Approach FY 04 Year 1	PPC Approach FY 05 Year 2	PPC Approach FY 04 Year 1
ICU Admissions (n)	1753	1798 (+45)	1820 (+76)	1094
Atlas Severity Grade	1.9	2.0	2.1	2.2
Age (years)	62 (24-80)	62 (50-74)	65 (39-71)	64 (56-76)
Gender (M/F)	22/15	3/3	4/7	1/2
Central lines deployed (n)	1110	1321* (211)	1487* (377)	1518*
Line-days	4687+	5052*	6705*	6072*
Infections	49	6*	11*	3*
Patients Infected	37	6*	11*	3*
Rates (infections/ 1000 line-days)	10.5	1.2*	1.6*	0.49*
Deaths	19 (51%)	1 (16%)*	2 (18%)*	0 (0%)*
Reliability (# of lines placed to get 1 infection)	22	185*	135*	506*

3. *Create a National Commission on Health Care Payment with two charges: A) End the profound cynicism of the healthcare pricing system; B) Fix the payment system to eliminate disincentives to "do the right thing."*

Once we have a map of the way forward, making sure that how we pay for healthcare services helps us and doesn't hurt us is the next step. I would give a National Commission on Health Care Payment six months to produce action recommendations to Congress and the President necessary to solve the dysfunctions in how we bill and reimburse for health care services.

A. A destructive pricing and billing system

Health care is the only industry that keeps two sets of books as a matter of course. The set of bills that are sent out by hospitals and others are a fiction. Contracts with insurers pay only a fraction of the listed price. Unless, that is, you don't have insurance. In that case, you're asked to pay full price. In Pennsylvania in 2004, hospitals were reimbursed 28.7 cents for every dollar they "billed." This was the exact rate of reimbursement they expected.

In addition to raising obvious issues of equity, this creates terrible problems on at least two other fronts.

First, it consumes enormous resources throughout the system in a shell- game that destroys value rather than creating it. Hospitals are obsessed with exploiting loop-holes in their contracts with insurers and the federal government to "optimize" revenue, producing ever-more complicated and fictitious pricing schemes and "black box" financing systems that not only profoundly distract health care managers from actually delivering a better product, but actually add complexities and distortions that interfere with care.

For example, across the country, efforts to optimize revenue from radiology services have produced Byzantine billing codes that are overwhelming to the physicians that order them and the nursing floors that enter the orders, and so produce innumerable dropped and confused orders that are changed in radiology departments, producing frustration and negative impacts on patient care.

Second, in my experience, if you ask people to work every day in organizations where major facets of their work are fictions, it has a corrosive effect on the whole enterprise. If we are not forthright about something as fundamental as what we charge and why, it eats at our sense of excellence and integrity.

I don't understand how the health care professions themselves can live another year with the current system. And if you have not yet read the current issue of *Health Affairs*, which includes two devastating articles on the current state and evolution of the hospital pricing system, I recommend it to you and suggest that after reviewing it you, as stewards of our national interest, will not be able to live another year with the current system.

The President's push for transparency of health care pricing for consumers deserves strong support. Properly driven, the scrutiny that would follow disclosures would be extraordinary, and the broken health care pricing system couldn't withstand it.

B. Eliminate disincentives to "do the right thing" in our reimbursement systems

The failures of the health care payment system to reward health care providers for doing the right thing for patients, or performing at better levels than their competitors, are many. I'll point to just two fronts for rapid action.

First, the unsustainable pace of health care cost increases is driven in large part by the increasing burden of chronic diseases such as diabetes on the American population.

Today chronic disease accounts for 75% of all health care costs, according to the Institute of Medicine and the Centers for Disease Control and Prevention. In turn, combating chronic disease effectively requires much more effective primary and preventive care.

Yet, if you look at our payment systems, you will see that we are paying hundreds of millions of dollars every year for patients to undergo advanced procedures — many of which have been proven by the literature to be "washes" in whether they sustain life — while paying very poorly for effective primary care that would have helped stay the progression of the disease in the first place.

A recent in-depth story by *The New York Times* identified what drives this sad state of affairs. A primary cause is the reluctance of commercial health insurers to provide effective preventive and chronic care benefits for diabetics, for fear that they will attract a disproportionate share of persons with diabetes. The insurance market exists to spread financial risk efficiently, yet we have allowed it to evolve in ways that insurance companies are allowed to avoid risk, with terrible impacts on human suffering.

It doesn't have to be this way. Over the past five years, the Veteran's Administration shifted its resources sharply toward primary care. They held their cost of care constant per patient at a time when general healthcare costs increased 50%, and dramatically raised the quality of care provided to veterans (a quality which sharply exceeds the performance of the rest of the American health care system). In Pittsburgh, the VA increased primary care for diabetics and has seen a corresponding 38% reduction in foot amputations. Will Medicare, private insurers and large health care purchasers have the guts to follow the VA's lead? Surely this panel can see that they do.

Second, while the intellectual infrastructure to "pay for performance" is evolving, the government's and private market's embrace of this ability has been tepid at best. The quality incentive programs that exist are typically less than 1% of annual revenue for a hospital, when hospital CEOs will tell you that at least 5% would be required to "get their attention."

The Medicare/Medicaid program has launched a few payment experiments for physicians and hospitals, but they generally don't put enough revenue on the table to shift behavior. My staff can find only one physician group in the United States where it is possible for a doctor to make 30% more income by performing at the highest possible levels in the quality of care they provide their patients. The scale and scope of our so-called "pay for quality" efforts should be immediately and radically expanded.

4. Prejudice the health care system toward truth telling.

Rethinking our approach to medical malpractice is more important than the amount of assets it involves would suggest (perhaps 2% of direct health care spending). It should be a priority because the current system inhibits rapid learning from mistakes, which is the fastest and only way to radically improve all that ails our health care delivery processes.

Again, it is helpful to me to think of problems in terms of first principles.

> ***The first principle of health care for me is that patients should get the best possible quality of care, and should be absolutely safe.***

That means that when things go wrong, these incidents need to be exposed and learned from, immediately, so that they won't be repeated.

Putting in place systems to speed the open flow of information about errors, poor outcomes and solutions was an important component of how aviation, nuclear power and Alcoa became safe enterprises

It turns out that despite physicians' and hospitals' fears of lawsuits, openness about errors is what patients want most. A growing body of research and experience show that when something goes wrong, patients and their families want to feel like they've been leveled with, receive a full apology, and be assured that actions have been taken to prevent the same problem from happening to someone else. They are less likely to sue if they get those things than if they do not.

Toward a Blame-Free System

Two forces can be meshed to radically advance safety, quality, and efficiency.

First, health care needs a "blame-free" error learning system that can help health care workers learn from errors almost instantly across the country. Congress last year passed enabling legislation to create a national error reporting system that could fulfill this goal. I say "could" because a critical design decision remains.

It is critical that in the current regulation-writing phase, the learning system be structured to allow every health care professional to be able to access and learn from it on an around-the-clock "real time" basis, at the granular level of each incident (with measures taken to protect the privacy of patients and anonymity of particular institutions, of course).

It will be the tendency of bureaucrats, experts, and lawyers to restrict access to the database to a very few, who will scan for problems and issue periodic safety bulletins. Unfortunately, this approach doesn't work to produce safety in any complex organization or endeavor.

Each individual actor knows the nature and risks of their work and workplace the best, and holding them accountable for learning and allowing them to learn on a constant, specific basis is the proven way to make them capable and responsible for creating safety in their own work.

To make this system truly powerful for eliminating injury, however, requires turning the current medical malpractice system on its head. Congress should create a genuine economic incentive under medical liability laws for caregivers to use the error reporting system for learning and rapid application.

Here is what I propose.

If mistakes are reported to the learning system and the patient within 24 hours of discovery, and measures to prevent the error from happening again are installed within a week, payment to the patient could be limited to their economic damages with some basic adjustments for fairness. And those payments should be made by society, not individual providers.

If an error isn't reported promptly to the patient and the national learning system, however, the provider could be subject to treble damages.

This suggestion is something of a political inconvenience in the current political battle over medical malpractice in which neither side is proposing the right balance of relief and responsibility.

But evidence across a number of domains — including worker safety on a national basis and my own experience at Alcoa — suggest creating the right incentives and disincentives for learning are necessary to set the conditions for rapid, steady, sustainable improvements in safety. And I do think this could be a "breakthrough" approach to medical malpractice that moves us beyond the current stale posturing that is so tiresome to the American people and, I believe, each of you.

In Conclusion

To conclude, I want to reiterate the three major imperatives that face this Committee in health care.

First, stop tinkering at the margin of incorrectly characterized problems with tax policy, and attach the responsibility and resources for achieving equitable access to health care to each individual American.

Second, deploy the proven ideas and principles of systems analysis to make it possible to capture the 30%-50% improvements in value per dollar invested in healthcare that are clearly possible.

Third, use the same "return to first principles" approaches to address the other critical dilemmas facing this Committee, such as Social Security and an inequitable, unworkable tax system, and you will see mutually-reinforcing improvements in the social and financial condition of the American people.

It has been a privilege to share these prescriptions and the experiences that inform them with this Committee. Appendices with additional details on my recommendations follow. I would be happy to answer questions and continue the discussion as you move forward to address our most urgent national problems.

Appendices (1 and 2 are included below):

1. Total Value Opportunity Proposal-Senate Finance Committee
2. Healthcare Issue Brief: Transforming Medical Malpractice
3. "Truth in Medicine," Paul H. O'Neill, The Washington Post, December 24, 2004
4. "What Health Care Can Be," Paul H. O'Neill, Healthcare Financial Management, June 2005
5. "A New Idea for Social Security," Paul H. O'Neill, Los Angeles Times, February 15, 2005.

Appendix 1

TOTAL VALUE OPPORTUNITY PROPOSAL — SENATE FINANCE COMMITTEE

CORE IDEA OF THE PROJECT:

The Institute of Medicine reports and a wide range of other studies and reports have highlighted things gone wrong in the U.S. health and medical care sector. The evidence consistently suggests that major improvements in patient outcomes and the health care status of Americans could be achieved while reducing costs by 30–50%.

However, while there is a great deal of activity in response to these findings there is not much evidence of a significant improvement in patient outcomes, and cost increases continue unabated. Why?

Policy makers react to the aggregate evidence by seeking one or two major "levers" to radically improve the quality, safety and efficiency of care. But the problems of complex systems such as American health care delivery can not be solved by edict.

At the local level, practitioners believe their error rates are small, regrettable but largely inevitable, within the national norms, and that they are under-compensated and underappreciated for what they do. They are opposed to transparent identification and sharing of things gone wrong because of perceived legal risk.

Many see waste and aggravation in things they are required to do — filling out insurance forms, for example — but not many see opportunities for quality improvements and cost saving in things they believe they can control.

Both groups — policymakers and practitioners — would be guided toward more constructive action by the creation of a compelling "business case" for the application of quality ideas and principles in the health and medical care sector by specifying and quantifying the financial value associated with:

- Errors (e.g., extended stays associated with wrong medications or wrong procedures. Cost of injuries to staff; lost work days and restricted work)
- All repair activity (e.g., time spent clarifying illegible or incomplete medication and other doctors' orders)
- All non-value added activity (e.g., time spent searching for needed materials - - medications, equipment, supplies)

RELEVANCE OF THE PROBLEM AND PROPOSED INNOVATIONS:

The current problems of safety, quality and waste in the American health care system directly harm tens of millions of Americans each year and indirectly harm the interests of every American. The failure of policymakers and executives to understand how to address safety, quality and cost problems should now be the central focus in this arena. Practical, powerful diagnostic techniques proven to speed radical improvements in other large, complex, high-risk industries could be used to address this gap.

APPROACH AND METHODOLOGY:

Select and work with five high reputation hospitals to document the difference between current patient outcomes and cost performance and the potential results if the care process eliminated errors and the waste associated with system design inefficiencies.

Assemble a team of analysts with successful experience in using and deploying the ideas of systems analysis, six sigma, lean manufacturing, the Toyota Production System and activity-based costing. Over a period of twelve months, analyze all major pathways in the patient care process to produce the project objective.

INTENDED CHANGES IN HEALTH CARE:

To provide the operational facts that are needed to press for accelerated improvement in American health and medical care, by:

- Creating a greater public sense of urgency to change health care by showing specifically where value is being lost and providing a better set of tools to help the public understand how it might be accomplished.

- Providing health care executives a map of their core processes that highlights the problems that embed error and waste in the system, and provides targeted tools to help the executives eliminate those causes.

- Strengthening the will and fact base of policy makers and corporate purchasers to:
    - ○ Overhaul reimbursement systems to successfully reward value creating care.
    - ○ Recognize the areas in which well-intended rules and regulations are impeding progress toward safe and perfect care, and remove those impediments.

Appendix 2

Healthcare Issue Brief: Transforming Medical Malpractice

Prepared by:

Value Capture Policy Institute

If the purpose of the medical malpractice system is to provide a powerful incentive for health institutions and providers to eliminate error, the system has failed. Based on Lucien Leape's scholarly work, over 300 million medication errors occur each year. The Institute of Medicine estimates that between 50,000 to 98,000 deaths per year are attributable to medical errors. There are countless other measures of total system failure including never-ending streams of falls, empty oxygen tanks, and unmet patient needs.

These errors also have a steep economic cost, building rework and instability into the system and driving a substantial portion of the growth in health care spending.

When people who are injured are asked what they want of the system, the most common responses are:

1. To receive an apology for the harm that occurred.
2. To be told exactly what happened, immediately and with complete honesty.
3. To be assured that everything has been done to guarantee that the same problem won't victimize anyone else, and;
4. To receive full compensation for lost wages and medical costs.

Apart from failing to prevent harm, the current medical malpractice system fails to deliver any of these outcomes desired by victims of error. A simple analysis reveals why.

The malpractice system functions on the assumption that, if the punitive damages for harm are great enough, doctors, nurses, and hospitals will make every effort to avoid error. There are two fundamental problems with this logic. First, people working in health care are already doing everything they know to avoid errors, but the way the system is designed makes errors inevitable. Secondly, the people who are running health care organizations are functioning without the commodity they most need to solve these problems, information about the real root causes of these system errors.

The current medical malpractice system actually impairs the ability of health care leaders to offer patients the thing they most want, error-free care.

There is a rough parallel to this problem in the evolution of the worker's compensation system. By the early 1900s, thousands of workers were killed or maimed each year by industrial systems that were not designed for safety. As a direct result, businesses were bearing enormous legal costs defending themselves against numerous lawsuits. It led to a crushing insurance burden. Between 1911 and 1940, as the problem became a crisis for both workers and businesses, they agreed to legislative compromises in every state that addressed many of the system problems from a safety and a cost perspective.

Government required employers to buy insurance to offset the economic burden of medical costs for people who were hurt and could not work through the workers compensation system. In exchange for this reduction in legal exposure, companies were required to share information about every incident so that all employers could avoid similar events.

We propose a similar system for medical malpractice, upgraded based on current learning and technology. The federal government (or state governments as an at-scale laboratory) would set up a fund to pay the economic damages for patients harmed by the health care system in exchange for mandatory reporting of everything gone wrong and systemic actions to remedy problems that could cause harm. In return for this protection from liability, anyone failing to report an incident would be liable in the regular court system for treble or quadruple damages. Reporting could take place in a national, real-time database designed to make it easy for anyone to share problems in the system with the potential to cause harm. Additionally, anyone could look to this database to learn from root cause solutions shared there.

This system would allow people to reduce the medical malpractice problem by preventing recurring errors at their root rather than focusing on the financing. Most importantly, this proposal would remove blame from the culture and free health care systems to expose and learn from their mistakes in the pursuit of perfect patient care.

The Value Capture Policy Institute is a non-profit organization dedicated to advancing state and federal policies that create the conditions for every human need to be met without waste or error.

Questions for Reflection and Discussion

1. Describe a time in your career when you experienced what Paul "understood, and Wall Street didn't — that people will respond to a set of values and proven ideas and principles to produce unbelievable increases in performance." If you are unable to describe this experience, why do you think that is?

2. In what ways does benchmarking "accept a certain level of error or poor quality as 'normal'?" If your organization uses benchmarks to measure safety and quality, what steps

can you take to eliminate benchmark thinking and implement theoretical limit thinking?

Final Question

1. Is Habitual Excellence an abstract concept or concrete reality? How can your organization become habitually excellent?

Summary of the "Playbook"

By Mark Graban

When I first started studying Paul O'Neill's speeches, my one reaction was that he was laying out a playbook that could be used by leaders, especially by CEOs who were new to an organization, in any industry.

When I interviewed retired Alcoa executive Bill O'Rourke in our "Habitual Excellence" podcast series, he spoke of using O'Neill's "playbook" when he took the challenging opportunity to lead Alcoa's business in Russia.

O'Rourke said:

> ***"I think it's easier when you are new, because people will expect the change and you expect yourself to be a new leader and to drive change. But, it can also be done with existing leaders who have an enlightenment when they decide, now, I'm going to drive change in the organization."***

O'Rourke was able to follow O'Neill's playbook, which included starting with safety and aiming to be the best in the world at everything you do as an organization.

Across O'Neill's speeches, a playbook emerges; what follows is my attempt to summarize this playbook. The playbook is a system that is built on principles. If you don't share the principles (such as "nobody should ever get hurt at work") then I wouldn't expect his playbook to work for you and your team. If you try to copy just part of the system (setting a goal of zero), I also wouldn't expect this playbook to work.

Elements of the playbook include:

Make a commitment that nobody should get hurt at work (the same could be said about patients in a health system).

State that you want to be the safest company in the world (and the best at everything that you do).

Stop the use of the word "accident" (which makes it sound inevitable or something God wanted) and use the word "incident" instead.

Realize that only the leader, as CEO, can create the environment and the culture that allow people to do great improvement work and take action toward that end.

Recognize that it's a privilege to be in a position of leadership.

Visit sites and where the work is done and make these commitments to workers in person.

Say that you won't make anybody budget for safety improvement — you'll find a way to pay for it.

Give out your personal phone number and tell employees to CALL you if the safety commitment isn't being met by local managers.

When you get that first phone call, thank the employee and follow up immediately with the plant manager (or hospital CEO).

> Note: Word will spread that you are following up on your words with action — this will be a big benefit to your culture change efforts.

Set goals at the "theoretical limit" (such as zero harm) but do not "bludgeon" people with that goal — use it as an inspirational and aspirational goal.

Encourage root-cause problem solving instead of papering over problems.

Take away excuses, such as "it's not possible" and "it's not in the budget."

Practice extreme transparency with information across the organization, including reports about injuries that start with the worker's name (to humanize the situation and keep it from being just numbers).

Publish employee injury data publicly on the company website. State metrics in ways that are easy to understand — use the number of infections, not the rate of infections per thousand line-days, for example.

Establish a "real-time safety information system" where any injury is identified and recorded within 24 hours. Share this information with the entire organization.

Learn to "ask questions like a third grader" and to keep asking "why?"

Create a more egalitarian culture, for example questioning why executives get perks like free coffee and danish that are not offered to factory workers.

Focus on safety is something that everybody can commit to — it's "unarguable." You'll end up on the path to habitual excellence related to everything the business does.

I deeply admire the clarity of purpose that O'Neill had. I appreciate his playbook and his true respect for every employee, going beyond their physical safety. He wasn't just about words. He was also about acting on and leading according to his principles.

Questions for Reflection and Discussion

1. What elements of the playbook do you see that are missing from the list above?

2. What would your hypothesis or expectation be if your organization got a new CEO, hired from the outside, who articulated and followed this playbook?

3. Could a CEO who had been at an organization for a while suddenly start following this approach? What reaction would you expect from the organization? What challenges would the CEO face and how could they overcome?

About Value Capture

In 2005, Value Capture was founded with Paul O'Neill, former Alcoa CEO and US Treasury Secretary, whose innovative thinking made Alcoa the safest workplace in the world. As a consequence of this achievement, O'Neill realized another important outcome — an increase in the company's efficiency and profitability.

For over a decade, O'Neill's passion for improving healthcare safety and reducing healthcare costs has been channeled into the work at Value Capture, where the methodology has been honed.

Today, the distinguished team of advisors and thought leaders at Value Capture seeks to help you and your organization achieve habitual excellence via one unifying focus, one value-based structure, and one performance system. In other words, we help you capture dramatically more value through achieving perfect care and perfect safety for patients and staff.

We developed the approach with world leaders in quality, safety and profitability, inside and outside healthcare. Starting with some of the earliest proofs that perfect safety and financial gain go hand-in-hand in American hospitals, Value Capture has helped CEOs from community hospitals to the nation's largest academic medical centers to integrated delivery systems tailor the strategy to their unique circumstances to produce hardwired results.

Our principle-based methods are helping healthcare organizations across the country capture and sustain astonishing increases in safety, quality, efficiency and satisfaction, all while lowering costs.

To learn more, please visit our website: http://valuecapturellc.com/

We also invite you to:

- Listen to our podcast, "Habitual Excellence"
  - www.valuecapturellc.com/podcast

- Check out our YouTube channel
  - https://www.youtube.com/user/ValueCapture

- Follow and engage with us on Twitter and LinkedIn
  - www.twitter.com/valuecapture1

  - https://www.linkedin.com/company/value-capture-llc-value-capture-policy-institute/

Made in the USA
Monee, IL
04 October 2020